Fantasy Furniture

Fantasy Furniture

Text by Bruce M. Newman
and Alastair Duncan

RIZZOLI
NEW YORK

I dedicate this book to my father and mentor, Meyer, who, without an elementary-school education, founded Newel Art Galleries fifty years ago; and to my wife Judy and my daughter Emily, for giving me the love, motivation, and inspiration that one needs in life.

First published in the United States of America in 1989 by
RIZZOLI INTERNATIONAL PUBLICATIONS, INC.
300 Park Avenue South, New York, NY 10010

Library of Congress Cataloging-in-Publication Data

Newman, Bruce M.
Fantasy furniture.
Bibliography: p. 197
  1. Furniture—History—19th century—Themes, motives.
2. Furniture—History—20th century—Themes, motives.
3. Furniture—Styles. 4. Fantasy in art. I. Title.
NK2385.N49 1989 749.2'04 89-45424
ISBN 84-78-1119-0

Designed by Charles Davey
Set in type by Rainsford Type, Danbury, Connecticut
Printed and bound by Toppan Printing Co., Tokyo, Japan

FRONTISPIECE:
*Iconographic liberties were surely taken
in creating the carved top of this late-
nineteenth-century Chinese export armchair. It would be difficult to imagine a
Chinese symbol not included in this decorative scheme. Flower-filled vases,
dragons, equestrians, scholars bamboo,
and foliage abundantly adorn this hong
mu armchair.*

OPPOSITE:
*A late-Victorian cast-iron desk lamp,
circa 1900, draws it inspiration from
Renaissance metalwork. An adjustable
griffin-like bird, affixed to a standard
with a circular spreading foot, supports
a metal dome with a band of mythological arabesques, dolphins and figures.*

Contents

Foreword

ABOVE AND OPPOSITE:
This eccentric, late-nineteenth-century English Eastlake side chair is carved with a circular open back centering an exotic bird with well-carved plumage. The three-sided concave seat is raised on tapered legs headed by stylized incised lappets. This gilt incising is characteristic of Eastlake designs. It is upholstered in a printed floral cotton contemporaneous with the chair and inspired by the fabrics of William Morris.

Although it might seem that in modern times our furniture has been dictated by the Bauhaus and its offshoots—those almost pathologically serious "machines" for sitting, lounging, reclining, and working—it isn't altogether true. We are certainly dominated by the conglomeration of severe chrome tubes, meager leather patches, and artfully bent plywood or stiff slabs of minimalist metal but not totally done in by them. Emerging from the sleek contemporary, the tiresome "repros," and the tarted- and gussied-up antiques is a style of wit, irony, imagination, and fantasy. It's happening primarily in the crafts movement and suffers because it is made more to be looked at in exhibitions than actually used. But no matter—amongst the tubes and the traditional, fantasy is being born again.

There's something reassuring about being amused by furniture, by having it actually make you think and wonder. When was the last time a chair, a sofa, a highboy, a coatrack, or an umbrella stand made you chortle? A contemporary one, that is.

That there is so little fantasy furniture today and, until this book, so little scholarly attention devoted to the subject has, I think, a lot to do with the aesthetic self-consciousness that seems to have overcome us in the twentieth century. We are so edgy about making an aesthetic gaffe that we dare not laugh or even smile at something so socially "vital" as furniture. It's almost as if fine furniture is only there to collect, to admire, to identify as in a spotting test and thereby "ace" someone less knowledgeable, or is merely something to have published in an upmarket, sumptuously produced interior decorating magazine, most certainly not something to wink about or roar with laughter over.

Our forefathers had no such strictures or doubts. These days some of us tend to think of the Victorians who revered fantasy furniture as quaint or even corny and look upon the collectors of the eighteenth century as somehow jaded because of their frank appreciation of fantastic forms in furniture. Not at all! They were seldom corny and hardly ever jaded. They were confident, far more confident than we, knowing that humorous styles could also safely enter the gates of furniture heaven. In addition, having been educated in the liberal arts and the classics, they instantly "got the joke" when they saw the legs of a table that had marched out of mid-fourteenth-century manuscript marginalia, or masks, animals, and spiny shapes that had surfaced from the world of dreams. They recognized, smiled, and laughed.

The nice thing about the glorious objects depicted and discussed in this landmark volume is that they are once again, after a long time, emerging to make us crinkle our foreheads in wonder and allow us to become openly amused by their fantastical inventiveness.

THOMAS HOVING

A masterpiece of cabinetry, this late neo-classical pier table, created around 1825, is inlaid with a variety of exotic woods to form contrasting surfaces. The shaped marble top rests above a Gothic frieze carved with arches and mounted with pearls. The tapered supports are carved with winged dragons which rest on a leaf-carved plinth.

Preface

My infatuation with fantastical design began in 1950, when I accompanied my father on one of his antique-buying trips to England. He took me to Brighton to see the Royal Pavilion. It was a particularly memorable experience for me because my first impression upon entering that incredible building was that I had stepped into a surrealistic Land of Oz. Its decoration, with glittering riches presented in a whimsical fashion, tickled me so much, I thought I might be walking through a daydream. I knew then that I was attracted to unusual, amusing, and exotic furniture that seemed to have a sense of humor. I haven't forgotten the Brighton Pavilion, and my career as an antiquarian has been dedicated to pursuing and collecting furniture and objects that might feel at home there.

This book is not meant as a complete history of furniture. I have attempted, instead, to present, in an amusing and enlightening manner, examples of what I consider to be the more intriguing styles of what I like to call *fantasy furniture*. Very little is known about the Grotto, "Black Forest," Grotesque, Mythological, Horn, and Antler styles. Fascinating to look at, they arouse one's curiosity about their original intent and function. It has been quite gratifying to have researched and come up with some information regarding the growth and development of these period styles. We now know who designed many of these pieces, when they were made, and for whom they were created.

Prior to the mid-eighteenth century, most of the ornate carvings on furniture were only spiritual or symbolic in meaning. It was not until 1801, when the Prince Regent, along with his coterie of imaginative architects and designers, decided to enlarge and enhance his pavilion at Brighton, that a signal or license was given to the rest of society, allowing them to escape from conformity and become seduced by fantasy. I have focused the contents of this book on that particular period, because it was during those one hundred or so years (from 1800 to 1915) that furniture craftsmen and interior decorators produced the largest and richest number of examples of these exciting and magical styles.

There seems to be a renewed interest in fantasy furniture. It might well represent the desire of many members of our present society to again trade reality for the mystery of dreams.

BRUCE M. NEWMAN

Fathers of Fantasy

Fortunately, my business trips take me to many interesting locations around the world. Two of my favorite places to visit are the Royal Pavilion at Brighton, built by the Prince Regent, and Linderhof Castle in the Bavarian Alps, built by Ludwig II.

Although the English Prince Regent and Ludwig II of Bavaria never lived a day on earth together (since the Prince died in 1830 and Ludwig was born in 1847), the two were destined to have the greatest influence on the whimsical, exotic, and frivolous style of decorative art that blossomed in the nineteenth century. Their eccentric life-styles clearly illustrate how they both developed a powerful appetite for fantasy.

King George IV, better known as the Prince Regent, channeled all of his idiosyncrasies and his creative aesthetic sense into the design of the Royal Pavilion at Brighton. The robust splendor, the wild, dragonish decorative details, and the eclectic mixture of furniture made this building appear flushed with excitement and also made the Regency period the most richly imaginative era in the decorative arts.

As if on cue, Ludwig II appeared during the second half of the nineteenth century to continue the momentum of exotic grandeur. Indeed, he soon attained a reputation as "the fairy-tale king." He built "dream castles" as if building theaters to set a stage for his own world of illusions. Having lived most of his life in fear of crowds, he built surrealistic layers of insulation around himself like secret passageways to his own fantasy world. Both he and the Prince Regent were enchanted with quaint and amusing decorations, with which they could surround themselves and give substance to their dreams—often dreams of eliminating the outside world. These two men can unquestionably be called "the fathers of fantasy."

BRUCE M. NEWMAN

OPPOSITE:
A Chinese dragon painted in iron red, amid cloud bands on a blue-sky ground, provides the theme for the base of an ormolu-mounted porcelain candelabra from the Brighton Pavilion.

Painted canvas, cement, and complicated waterworks provide the backdrop for Ludwig II's magical Venus Grotto. Built in the 1870s outside Linderhof, it represents the "Venusberg" from the opera Tannhäuser. *The artificial grotto was a fairyland retreat where the king would lose himself in a dream world.*

In Western culture it has required privilege—wealth and rank, and lots of both—to allow one to flee life's real or imagined perversities by the creation of make-believe worlds. For most of mankind, the daily grind of work and survival preoccupies one to the point where, however much one might yearn for a similar escape, such aspirations remain unfulfilled. A cruel irony of life is that the creation of fantasy environments remains the preserve of those who need them least.

A survey of fantasy furniture must therefore focus initially on the attempts of history's aristocracy to build themselves imaginary kingdoms, which they have done largely by means of architectural follies, grottoes, and exotic palaces. Many of these demand appreciation for their sheer scale, ingenuity, and persistence in the pursuit of a fugitive dream.

In Italy, the gardens of Bomarzo, on the grounds of the Palazzo Orsini near Viterbo, have enthralled visitors since their creation in the 1570s. Gigantic mythological monsters, sphinxes, and truncated torsos evoke the inhabitants of our nightmares. To the north, on Isola Bella in Lake Maggiore, the erection of the Palazzo Borromeo consumed succeeding generations of one family for three hundred years, beginning in around 1630. An architectural folly, the palace resembles a ship anchored in the middle of the lake, taking its form from the legend that the Borromeos descended from pirates. In Sicily, a few miles from Palermo, the Villa Palagonia, an eighteenth-century palace, is crammed with objects of fantasy—statues of five-headed hydras, mirrors that distort the viewer's image, chairs studded with sharp spikes that prevent one from sitting, punchinellos, ostriches in hooped skirts, and lions dining with napkins—which together form a delightful Alice-in-Wonderland world of lunacy.

In the 1500s the archduke of Austria, Ferdinand II, built Ambras Castle in the mountains above Innsbruck, where he housed his painting collection of freaks of nature. A bearded female dwarf, who in real life married a man whose face was entirely covered in hair, stares out from one canvas. Legend records that she gave birth to a girl child with the head of an animal. Nearby showcases house a collection of bezoars—concretions found in camels' stomachs—which were used as talismans in pagan rituals. In Wiltshire, England, in the early 1800s, William Beckford hedged his bets by creating two architectural follies at Fonthill Abbey; one to realize his worldly political ambitions and the other, with its superimposed towers, to allow him to escape reality by gazing at the heavens, like an oriental potentate, contemptuous of his fellow mortals, in whom he feigned total disinterest. The United States largely missed out on the fantasy mania until the 1920s, when William Randolph Hearst, the newspaper tycoon, built Casa Grande near San Simeon, where he entertained Hollywood celebrities and other luminaries. Though erected on a scale that would have impressed even the fictional Gatsby, and jammed with lavish furnishings, the building startles the eye more than it triggers the imagination.

Fascination with the Orient has for centuries inspired Asian-style structures in Europe, notably Drottningholm, the Swedish royal palace six miles from Stockholm, built by Adolphus Frederick in the 1750s. In

Germany, Nymphenburg, the palace of the electors of Bavaria, and Schwetzingen, near Baden, both have exotic gardens, as does Hellbrunn Castle near Salzburg, Austria. By the late 1800s there were several other edifices in Europe from which one could draw inspiration for an exotic replica of one's own, including a Japanese house in Dresden and a Chinese pavilion in Potsdam, plus dozens of oriental teahouses. All of these pale in comparison with the Royal Pavilion in Brighton, however, which was created by the English Prince Regent, undisputedly the world's first modern father of fantasy.

None who have walked in wonderment through Brighton Pavilion would challenge this claim. The Pavilion's dazzling splendor overpowers today's visitor as much as it did the Prince's guests even while it underwent thirty-five years of protracted transformation—from 1791 to 1826—when, as George IV, he settled his court fully in London. The lavish mix of dragons, serpents, domes, and minarets rivals Marco Polo's description of the fabled pleasure dome of Xanadu, captured for posterity by Coleridge in his epic poem, "Kubla Khan, or a Vision in a Dream."

To comprehend fully the architecture and decor of the Royal Pavilion, it is necessary first to focus on the Prince Regent himself. What dreams and idiosyncracies drove him to such a pageant of exotic colors and architectural styles? The basic answer is that he could not live in a building without letting his imagination begin to work on it. His spurts of creativity, however, were interspersed with the romantic interludes and financial crises that punctuated his life successively as Prince of Wales, Prince Regent, and George IV. Indeed, his flights of fancy must be considered within the context of the rest of his life, which both on a personal and public level was seldom less than turbulent. Increasingly, he fled into a world of private dreams and visions—personified by the buildings in which he lived—which were the only meaningful part of his existence, one in which he increasingly sought refuge from public derision.

On turning twenty-one, the Prince Regent, on the invitation of his uncle, the duke of Cumberland, visited Brighton. He found the blend of gaiety and discretion to his liking, so he and his consorts settled on it as their playground. Not a natural seaside idyll, the town had first come to fame and fashion through the salesmanship of a Dr. Russell, from Lewes, who marketed the medicinal virtues of its seawater. A cold dip, it seemed, provided remedies for that female frailty, the vapors, especially if it was taken at hideously inconvenient times, such as before dawn in February. Sea bathing or drinking also encouraged fertility in young matrons; its advocates claimed that it was "better even than the mud of the Nile."

In 1802 the gift of some Chinese wallpaper—presented no doubt because the Prince had created a chinoiserie room in his London residence, Carlton House, the previous year—spurred his idea for two Chinese-inspired rooms in the Royal Pavilion: a gallery and a room with painted glass walls that gave the viewer the impression of standing inside a Chinese lantern. Gradually, the ambition to transform his princely seaside villa into a rich and Aladdinlike oriental palace preoccupied the Prince. Financial vicissitudes stalled the completion of his goal, but with the formal announcement in 1811 of George III's madness, he became

ABOVE:
George IV's fascination with exotica is illustrated in this cartoon, which depicts the king and Lady Conyngham atop a hybrid animal, given to him by the pasha of Egypt in 1827.

RIGHT:
This aquatint represents the west façade of George IV's Pavilion at Brighton. The minarets, chimney stacks, arched windows, and trellised balconies designed by Nash attest to the rage for exotic decor in England during the early part of the nineteenth century.

The COURT at Brighton à la Chinese !!

LEFT:
"The Court at Brighton à la Chinese" is the title of this cartoon, which depicts the Prince Regent seated on an overstuffed cushion. His daughter and her future husband are by his side, presenting a list to his ambassador to China of the items needed to finish the interior decoration of the Pavilion.

king in all but name, which enabled him, as regent, to gain access to the royal treasury. This allowed him to build as never before, with the assistance now of John Nash, whom he appointed surveyor-general in 1815. By now, he had rejected both his morganatic wife, Mrs. Fitzherbert, a second time, and his forced bride, Princess Caroline of Brunswick. Gross in size and wandering in mind, he retreated increasingly into a private dream world, prone to invalidism and flights of fantasy. The need to express himself through building and interior decorating became his saving grace. Pretense became reality as the Royal Pavilion, and to a lesser extent Buckingham Palace and Windsor Castle, came to manifest his ability to create some of England's proudest and most original architecture.

The Prince Regent's fantasies in Brighton were realized in two giant interiors, the Banqueting and Music rooms, both designed by Nash between 1817 and 1820, although a restrained exoticism persists throughout the more conventional areas of the Pavilion, including the corridor, north and south drawing rooms, salon, and bedrooms. A great deal of the furnishings, provided by Frederick Crace & Sons in the early 1800s, are made of real and simulated bamboo. A "bamboo" staircase balustrade even reveals itself, on inspection, to be made of painted cast iron.

Reached through the Octagonal Hall, with its delicate tented ceiling, then via the Entrance Hall and corridor (the latter the most persistently Chinese part of the Pavilion), the Banqueting Room comes as a *coup d'oeil*. Decorated by Robert Jones, who was responsible for the execution of the Prince's visions, it is among the most exhilarating sights in the world. It is dominated by a central dome ornamented in partial relief with the leaves of a plantain tree, from which is suspended a giant chandelier. An enormous silvered and winged dragon hovers at the apex of the chandelier, clutching in its claws the top of a light fixture. Weighing a ton and measuring thirty feet in height, with upturned lotus-leaf shades above a central beaded crystal fixture, the chandelier was lit by the new marvel, gas. In the corners of the room, smaller gasoliers, suspended from *fums,* Chinese mythological birds, were embellished with matching lotus-leaf shades. Around the room's perimeter, beneath a set of clerestory windows, serpents and dragons share duties with gilded dolphins as furniture capitals and supports, decorative accents to murals depicting formal groups of Chinese figures. Standing today in the midst of such resplendence, it is easy to imagine the room's original ambience, when the Prince Regent, overindulged, advancing in age, and flanked by twenty or so of his faithful roués, gorged himself on wine and the gargantuan piles of food sent through from the vast kitchen, where the celebrated French chef, Carême, marshalled a platoon of sweating cooks and scullions.

After dinner, guests were ushered into the Pavilion's second great wonder, the Music Room, where they were entertained with concerts in which Rossini and Kelby sang and the Prince himself rendered ballads in a proud baritone now a little uncertain with age and drink. The room was designed more for the eye than the ear, however, its walls enriched with serpents writhing headfirst down columns dividing great crimson-and-gold lacquered murals painted with chinoiserie confections. Above, a convex octagonal cove suspended chandeliers fashioned into monumen-

tal Chinese water lilies. Everywhere flying dragons and imaginary creatures abound, adding further magic to the fairy-tale spectacle.

The Prince found this rampant chinoiserie too light and trifling for the Pavilion's exterior. In addition, the style was now somewhat outmoded, as different manifestations of it had been in vogue in interior decoration for years. Something quite novel was required. For this, Nash adopted the Indian influence found in a handful of English buildings at the time, especially on the façade of Sezincote, a Gloucestershire mansion designed by the style's foremost proponent, S. P. Cockrell. Unlike Sezincote, though, which represented a formal translation of Indian architecture, Nash opted for a diluted Hinduism, to which he added hints of neo-Gothicism and the Moresque in the Pavilion's quatrefoils, battlements, and fretwork tracery. Beneath all the whimsy, in fact, the fine proportions and elegance of Henry Holland's 1787 classical Georgian villa are still discernible. The result was a building that baffled the understanding as much as it stimulated the imagination, a dream belonging to the Prince's search for a smart originality with which to astonish his circle of royal chums.

The Prince Regent had a formidable successor in King Ludwig II of Bavaria, whose eccentricities rivaled, if not exceeded, those of the English monarch. Known as the "dream king," "swan prince," or, less kindly, as "mad Ludwig," Ludwig succeeded to the Bavarian throne on the death of his father, Maximilian II, in 1864, at the age of eighteen. Overly shielded in his childhood from the responsibilities of the sovereignty he was to inherit, the naive youngster nevertheless attempted to administer the daily

ABOVE:
The gold-leaf and red-lacquer dragons on the cornice over the door in the Music Room of the Pavilion resemble the pagoda roofs of many Chinese temples. The trompe l'oeil dragons are taken from Chinese legends and are featured throughout the Pavilion.

ABOVE:
Guests standing beneath the succulent leaves and gilt dragon on the ceiling of the Banqueting Room may have pondered their whereabouts.

ABOVE:
Upon entering the Banqueting Room, the king's guests would immediately be drawn to gaze up at the ceiling. The large trompe l'oeil painting, with its grand plantain leaves and pendant gilt dragon surmounting a huge chandelier, is among the most extraordinary in the world.

affairs of state to the best of his ability but was increasingly disillusioned by the day-to-day machinations of his ministers. These included the expulsion from Munich of Richard Wagner, whom Ludwig had idolized since he attended a performance of *Lohengrin* in 1861. This adolescent adulation for the composer and his music continued throughout Ludwig's life, later manifesting itself in the themes with which he decorated several of his royal homes. Increasingly, the young king lingered outside the capital to escape the political intrigues and quarreling of his court. The short but fateful war with Prussia in 1866 left Bavaria with monumental damages to men, material, and property. Over thirty-million Gulden was paid to Prussia for reparations, alienating Ludwig further. From this time his absenteeism from Munich grew, generating the first rumors of a reclusive, "fairy-tale" monarch. Stories of solitary nocturnal sleigh rides through the lower Alps began to circulate among his subjects.

Like the Prince Regent, Ludwig found solace and self-fulfillment in architecture. Unlike him, however, he was not dependent on a vengeful father for funding. In 1867 he executed his first building, the Winter Garden, on top of his apartment in the Munich *Residenz*. Complete with a lake and boat, tropical vegetation, and an oriental kiosk with a Himalayan backdrop painted by Christian Jank, the venture anticipated the more fanciful and grandiose projects to follow. Several of these were never realized. Included was a plan to build a new Versailles, called *Meicost Ettal,* an anagram of Louis XIV's notorious dictum, *L'Etat c'est moi,* Ludwig's intended shrine to Bourbon absolutism and, specifically, to the Sun King, to whom he claimed a direct link through god-parentage. Land for *Meicost Ettal* was purchased in 1869, but this palace was never built. Another abortive venture was the plan for a Chinese Palace, to be built by the remote Plansee Lake. The most exhilarating unrealized project was Falkenstein, a Byzantine-inspired Rhineland fortress, which Ludwig planned to erect on an even more lofty and spectacular mountain aerie than Neuschwanstein, discussed below.

Of the three major residences that Ludwig did build—Neuschwanstein, Linderhof, and Herrenchiemsee—Neuschwanstein was the first (begun in 1868) and by far the most dramatic, transposing viewers into a bygone fantasy world. Perched on a rocky crag southeast of Hohenschwangen, the castle, complete with medieval towers and turrets, became the inspiration for Disneyland's Magic Kingdom. The interior, designed mainly by Julius Hofmann, included two extraordinary rooms: a bedroom in the late Gothic style and a Byzantine Throne Room derived from Edouard Ille's design for a hall of the Holy Grail.

By 1870 Ludwig had closed the door on normalcy, leaving himself free to pursue an alternative reality, one filled with the phantasmagoria of his own creation. In the same year he began his second royal retreat, Linderhof, a Trianon-type eighteenth-century villa. Far less picturesque than Neuschwanstein, Linderhof's fascination lies in its bizarre interiors. Foremost among these is the Venus Grotto. Inspired both by Capri's Blue Grotto and the Venus Grotto where Tannhäuser drank the cup of oblivion, Ludwig constructed his imitation rocky cavern out of canvas, cast iron, and cement. Against a giant backdrop painting depicting Tannhäu-

ABOVE:
Stalactites and the king's pleasure boat are prominent features in the tunnel-of-love-like blue caverns that wind their way through the Venus Grotto.

ABOVE:
This imaginative painting of Neptune's barge, created by the theater designer Franz Seitz, is one of numerous mythological and romantic subjects and scenes depicted throughout the many castles and retreats of Ludwig II.

LEFT AND BELOW:
This chair and candelabrum, made from coral, were designed by Seitz as accessories for the king's pleasure during his walks through the Venus Grotto.

ser's dalliance with the goddess of love, artificial stalactites framed a lake on which floated the royal shell-shaped barque. A small wave-making machine added reality. The theatrical effect was further heightened by kaleidoscopic lighting powered by Bavaria's first electric dynamo. Ludwig inaugurated his subterranean theater-in-the-round in solitude in 1877, on his thirty-second birthday. Certainly no other setting could have provided its creator with a more illusory world in which to toast his self-imposed exile.

Aboveground, Linderhof boasted some of Ludwig's most lavish room settings. Notable in a primarily rococo interior was the dining room, in the center of which stood an oval *Tischlein-deck-dich* (a table that sets itself) that was raised through the floor, fully spread, to enable Ludwig to dine in total privacy. The table was set for four celebrated ghostly dinner guests—Mme. Pompadour, Mme. de Maintenon, Louis XIV, and Louis XV—with whom the host conversed in French during his nightly repasts.

Two pavilions on the Linderhof grounds—a Moorish kiosk replete with a peacock throne and a Moroccan house, purchased directly from the 1878 Paris Exposition, in which Ludwig liked to dress in oriental costumes and smoke a chibouk—added a rich exoticism to the bewildering diversity of French furnishings and German mythological paintings in the main building.

For the site of his third castle, begun in 1878, Ludwig chose the island of Herren in Lake Chiemsee, an alpine setting with spectacular vistas. Herrenchiemsee was the realization of his earlier attempt to create a second Versailles. It was also a tribute to his idol, Louis XIV, and, by extension, an evocation of a glorious era when monarchs ruled by divine right, unaccountable to nineteenth-century ministers of state with niggling daily demands. Though more resplendent even than Linderhof in its gilded neo-rococo interiors, the building lacked the personal touches and idiosyncracies that characterize Ludwig's other residences. The magnificent bedroom and the great Hall of Mirrors—the latter a copy of the Galerie des Glaces in Versailles—lack originality and charm in their slavish re-creation of the French prototype. The sheer scale of ornamentation shows, though, that Ludwig's earlier attempts to stay close to his budget were now fully abandoned, resulting in a financial burden that his family had to assume on his mysterious death by drowning in 1886.

Today, the Prince Regent and King Ludwig are judged far differently than they were by their contemporaries. Time has eased the memory of their troubled kingships, leaving only the legacy of their architectural accomplishments. These prove that, despite their many inadequacies, both achieved a high measure of professionalism as builders. The enraptured throngs of tourists who now flock to Brighton and southern Bavaria annually show that the need to escape reality remains a fundamental part of human existence. It is quite likely that most of us, given the equal privilege of rank and wealth afforded the two monarchs, would attempt something similar: the creation of a gentler world in which dream and reality could become one.

ABOVE:
Having shut out reality, Ludwig would sail through the passages of his secret world in boats similar to this putto-driven, shell-shaped barge.

OPPOSITE:
Franz Seitz's design for a peacock throne inspired the Parisian designer Le Blanc-Granger to execute this throne, which now sits in the Moorish kiosk outside Linderhof. This exotic, Eastern-influenced throne, with its jeweled trappings, mystical beasts, and peacock plumage, would have been as suitable for the king of Siam or a Mogul prince.

OPPOSITE AND RIGHT:
This charming pair of demonic torchères may represent the Devil and his wife. Each well-carved walnut figure, dressed in tightly clad, late-nineteenth-century attire, extends an arm, which may have once held a tray. Their creator, possibly a Frenchman, took an additional liberty by carving the lower half of the Devil in the form of a mythological satyr.

Grotesque & Mythological

Throughout history, furniture has taken its inspiration from nature and animal forms. Egyptian inventiveness first supplied the impetus for the bizarre shapes and designs that embellished furniture in ancient times. Religious symbols and animal heads and feet, most notably bulls' hooves and lions' paws, were integrated into chair designs. Without realizing it, sixty years ago in the farm cottage where we lived, our first acquisitions were all related to animals. We purchased benches with lion heads, chairs with animal feet, porcelain birds on hoops, small animal ornaments, mirrors with eagle tops, and other furniture decorated with serpents and other creatures.

In the sixteenth century the "grotesque" form of design was characterized by incongruous combinations of monstrous or exaggerated natural forms. Inspiration was freely and uncritically drawn from an eclectic range of sources, including mythology. The designs and styles of these objects reflected the character and aspirations of the times. Amusements during the seventeenth and eighteenth centuries were few in comparison to those in the Victorian era. The *nouveaux riches* during this period delighted in bizarre and eccentric novelties with which they could vaunt their financial status. During this period there was also a return to the love of melodrama. Furniture was exaggerated in scale and curvature and greatly distorted. Craftsmen devoted themselves to these unique objects, which charmed their owners with fanciful, whimsical, and often bizarre forms. The fact that most, if not all, of the objects were poorly designed and unsuitably adapted to the other objects in an interior was largely ignored by patrons.

I have always enjoyed decorating with interesting furniture and often use an amusing decorative piece to add a sense of humor to the job.

Sister Parish

SISTER PARISH

Furniture has always reflected the character and aspirations of its time, revealing its existence at the dawn of civilization in the objects excavated from the tombs of ancient Sumer and Egypt. One hundred years before the discovery of Tutankhamen in 1922, couches and throne chairs jeweled and gilded with fantastic mythological birds and beasts—divine guardians for the journey of Egypt's royal dynasty through purgatory—emerged from the sands of the Nile to seduce the Western world with visions of spectacularly rich and heavenly kingdoms. This bright pageantry, which had provided the citizens of ancient Egypt with a sense of the physical and economic security needed for their monarchs to pass to the next world, generated an endless source of inspiration for early-nineteenth-century artist-designers and cabinetmakers in search of fresh forms of decoration. The brilliant palette and mythology inspired a host of furnishings, the first in the cycle of Egyptian revivalism that has continued until today.

Practically no records have survived of *any* furniture, let alone examples that merit interest in terms of the unusual, from the birth of Christendom through the Middle Ages. For more than a millenium furniture was rudimentary and sparsely decorated; neither local pagan superstitions, the satanic fabrications of itinerant storytellers, nor unexplained acts of nature conspired to create an innovative furniture style. For this, civilization had to wait considerably longer, almost to the birth of the Renaissance.

In the late Middle Ages, archaeological excavations in Rome unearthed a cache of artifacts that had been buried for aeons in the Eternal City's past. These finds were popularly known as *grotesques* after the subterranean ruins, or *grotte,* in which they were discovered. Renaissance artists and artisans drew eagerly on the iconography of these objects, which received formal artistic sanction with Raphael's inclusion of several in a Vatican commission in 1516. From this, their popularity spread rapidly throughout Europe, where they developed regional characteristics. Flemish and Dutch grotesque pattern books helped further to proliferate the popularity of the genre, until it was absorbed into all disciplines of the decorative arts. By 1612 the grotesque was sufficiently established for Peachman to offer the following description of it in his *Graphice:* "An unnatural or unorderly composition for delight's sake, of men, beasts, birds, flowers, etc., without Rime or Reason."

Renaissance grotesque ornament was included on all manner of fantastic creations, reflecting both man's hopes and fears. A menacing menagerie of griffins (themselves hybrids comprised of eagles' heads and wings with lions' bodies), sea dragons, and giant predatory birds were joined in bizarre configurations with sirens and exaggerated human forms. The original religious symbolism of these images gave way increasingly to a purely decorative one as they came to serve as secular accents, both on furniture and in the realm of architecture, where they were transformed into relief masques and gargoyles for building façades and corbels. In furniture, grotesque ornamentation served the Renaissance mercantile classes well in their need to vaunt their prosperity. Monumental pieces,

boldly carved and polychromed (and often far less comfortable than impressive), served notice of their owner's newfound affluence and emerging political power. The mix of indigenous and exotic influences, particularly in the traditional seafaring nations of Italy and Spain, provided a rich and highly theatrical mix of motifs in which formal cornucopia, dolphins, and lyres shared duty with bright exotic creations. These, in combination, replaced classical caryatids and terms as furniture supports.

Grotesques gained renewed popularity beginning in 1800, after Napoleon's Egyptian campaign, which galvanized the world of fashion with its rediscovery of pharaonic culture. Antiquity was suddenly awakened from its long sleep as Europe's archaeologists joined the race to rediscover man's origins. Beautiful and mysterious objects surfaced, nourishing the public's curiosity and love of romance. From Egypt came the Rosetta Stone and the first of Cleopatra's Needles (obelisks), from Greece the Elgin Marbles, and from Pompeii, in 1812, a lavish publication by F. Mazois in which watercolors of frescoes captured the exquisite beauty of the city's remote artistic heritage.

A predictable rash of classical revival styles followed, many loosely termed *Grecian,* whether they came from Greece, Italy, or the Levant. A corresponding nineteenth-century grammar of decorative ornament evolved as ancient civilization was scoured for its most fanciful imagery. Much of this found its way in France onto Napoleon III and Second Empire furnishings, and in England, onto the Victorian equivalent.

The solemnity afforded the early archaeological findings by the public—excavated artifacts were initially perceived as a type of mortuary art and therefore portentous and sacred—gradually gave way to a less reverent perception as the iconographies of different cultures from through-

out history were scrambled together, often indiscriminately. In the 1830s the English critic, Miss Mitford, noted the obvious dangers of a rampant eclecticism in her discussion of Rosedale Cottage, which she found

...overdone with frippery and finery, a toy-shop in action, a Brobdingnagian baby-house. Every room is in masquerade: the salon, Chinese, full of jars and mandarins and pagodas; the library, Egyptian, all covered with hieroglyphics, and swarming with furniture crocodiles and sphynxes. Only think of a crocodile couch and a sphynx sofa! They sleep in Turkish tents,

and dine in a Gothic chapel.... Now English ladies and gentlemen in their everyday attire look exceedingly out of place amongst such mummery...

Needless to say, the boundaries of good taste were violated with impunity in pursuit of ever-more exuberant forms of artistic expression.

One would do well to note the obvious in a study of furniture that sparks the imagination: It is invariably someone else's culture that conjures up images of the exotic and fantastic. A carved and gilded Chinese dragon, for example, can be unfamiliar and spectacular to the Western eye, but it is routine in the country of its origin. Equally important is the perspective that time affords one's view of an object. The iconography of one generation appears mundane and unfashionable to the next, but later its initial uniqueness and appeal again appear fresh. Victorians growing up in homes decorated by their parents with antler furniture, for example, probably perceived it primarily as uncomfortable (if not sharp and dangerous) and, in a negative sense, rustic. Time has softened that view: Antler furniture is now seen as quaint, innovative, and witty, qualities that receive high marks in an assessment of what is needed to make today's home livable and enjoyable. When judiciously used, grotesque and mythological decoration provide the same effect.

This pair of Egyptianesque painted and parcel-gilt armchairs, made in the 1920s, were inspired by the archaeological discovery of Tutankhamen's tomb. The rectangular back, carved with lotus blossoms, supports a winged uraeus. This serpent deity, called Netjer-ankh, *would have assisted Tutankhamen in his journey to the underworld. Also of note are the arms, which terminate in servants' heads.*

This unusual ebonized and giltwood three-fold screen is an Egyptophile's adaptation of a painting presumably seen while touring the Valley of the Kings. The staff bearers relate directly to freestanding figures found during the excavation of Tutankhamen's tomb. These figures are meant to flank the entrance to the underworld or protect the portal of his tomb.

LEFT:
This pair of Egyptian walnut and inlaid ivory lion stools was made in the late nineteenth or early twentieth century for the British market. They were probably placed near an entrance door to keep evil spirits away.

BELOW:
Pedestal stands in the form of acrobats were common in Italy as far back as the seventeenth century. This pair was made in Venice during the nineteenth century. Each double-jointed acrobat dressed in an Egyptian kilt balances precariously on his hands.

An Egyptian-revival painted walnut arm-chair, circa 1925, this stylized funerary or game chair depicts a lotus blossom and peacock's tail flanked by watchful heads. The arms terminate in an Udjat eye. The Udjat was a popular amulet in ancient Egypt. It symbolized piety, offered protection against sickness, and was thought to possess the power to restore the dead to life.

ABOVE:

Inspired by the late-eighteenth-century designs of Georges Jacob, this nineteenth-century Louis XVI-style side chair has a hoop-shaped back with a leaf-tip border and the circular, turned, stop-fluted legs frequently associated with Jacob. The prominently displayed peacock was a nineteenth-century innovation.

LEFT:

The Indonesian fourfold lacquer screen shown here is decorated with peacocks amid exotic foliage. During the nineteenth century, red-and-black lacquer screens of this type were commonly used by Asians and Europeans alike.

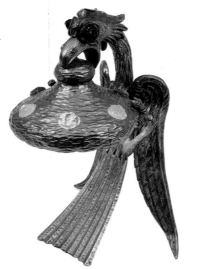

ABOVE AND LEFT:
A French giltwood side chair with an exuberantly carved open back of pierced C-scrolls and foliage, this piece attests to the mid-nineteenth-century exploitation and exaggeration of an earlier eighteenth-century design. Of particular charm is the seated monkey playing the flute. Based on early-eighteenth-century engravings, this singerie may have been adopted from an ormolu mount designed by the well-known eighteenth-century maître *Charles Cressent.*

A Florentine silver-gilt pedestal table possibly from the workshop of Andrea Baccetti. This truly exotic piece has an oval top carved to simulate the feathers of a pair of peacocks, which surmount the top. The stumplike support sprouts leaves and rests on a rock-carved base.

RIGHT:
This nineteenth-century Florentine peacock-form armchair is painted in tones of red and blue on a silver ground. It may be from the workshop of Andrea Baccetti.

OPPOSITE:
Presumably carved as part of a larger suite by Andrea Baccetti, this unique Florentine "silvered" settee takes the form of two peacocks with outstretched wings.

ABOVE, LEFT:
This demonic walnut coatrack is extremely well carved and more sculptural than utilitarian. It is without a doubt a one-of-a-kind masterpiece. Probably Italian and from the nineteenth century, it takes the form of a devilish beast, its serpent's tail entwined around a stump.

LEFT:
Japanese metalworkers were extremely prolific during the second half of the nineteenth century. This patinated bronze sculptural group depicts two woodland hermits, each clad in a leaf-sheathed kilt, supporting a beehive-shaped bell cast with cloud bands and stylized foliage. It may once have served to call monks to prayer.

ABOVE:
*An English nineteenth-century outdoor
settee features supports cast to simulate a
pair of grimacing dragons.*

ABOVE:
*Typically Venetian in design, this shell-
and dolphin-carved walnut piano stool is
yet another decorative object based on
earlier-eighteenth-century baroque and
rococo motifs. It is possible that the piano
was similarly carved.*

ABOVE AND OPPOSITE:
*A cane or umbrella stand made in Europe
during the nineteenth century, this piece
takes the form of a heron amid rocks,
grasping in its beak a snake which coils to
form a ring. It is realistically carved in walnut and has glass-inset eyes.*

This wildly imaginative, well-made lacquer desk is fitted with a superstructure carved with Chinese motifs. The variously sized cabinets, shelves, and drawers, surmounted by temple pediments carved with mythological beasts and painted with exotic foliage, surround a charming garden with a footbridge, set in a mountain landscape. Possibly an exhibition piece, it may also have been a gift to a foreign dignitary.

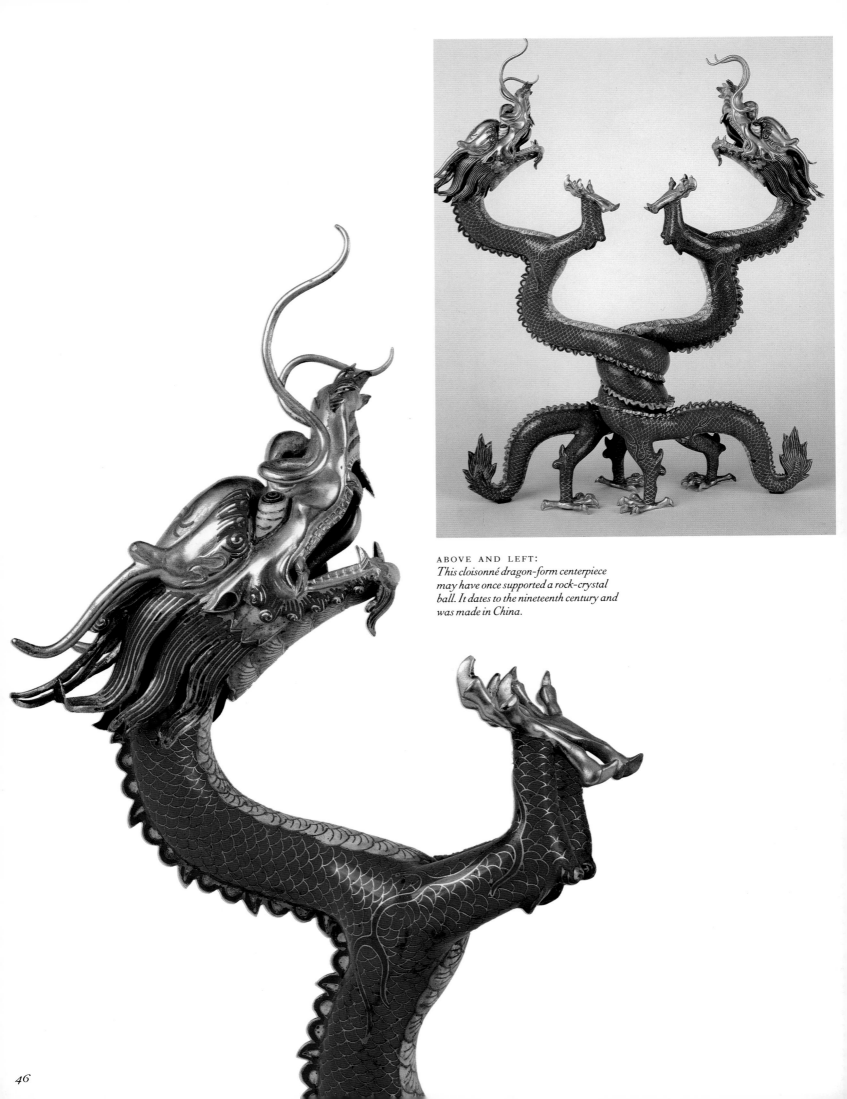

ABOVE AND LEFT:
This cloisonné dragon-form centerpiece may have once supported a rock-crystal ball. It dates to the nineteenth century and was made in China.

The three entwined dragons in this late-nineteenth-century Chinese candelabrum are decorated with multicolored enamel. This type of decoration, commonly called cloisonné, is made by pouring enamel paste between raised metal bands applied to the surface of the object.

Devils and demonic beasts were a popular subject matter for decorative whimsies. In this Continental bronze oil lamp made at the turn of this century, two winged beasts surround a standard with two domed shades. Resting atop the cresting is what appears to be the Devil himself.

ABOVE, LEFT:
This demonic walnut coatrack is extremely well carved and more sculptural than utilitarian. It is without a doubt a one-of-a-kind masterpiece. Probably Italian and from the nineteenth century, it takes the form of a devilish beast, its serpent's tail entwined around a stump.

BELOW:
This early- to mid-nineteenth-century fernery sports a black lacquer bowl resting on a baluster standard, surrounding three sea serpents with gilded featherlike tails and scale-carved bodies. It is a reminder of the whimsical tastes of the nineteenth-century European bourgeoisie.

RIGHT:
Ferneries and plant stands, though relatively mundane and domestic artifacts, provided nineteenth-century craftsmen with "canvases" on which to create works of art. In this Italian example, a gilded mythological serpent twists around an elongated stump, which supports a shell-like shelf.

49

RIGHT:
This "antique" patinated bronze brazier, cast in the form of three virile adolescent satyrs, supports a circular basin similar to many "excavated" at Pompeii. It dates from the nineteenth century and would have been a suitable prop in many neoclassical paintings.

RIGHT:
A product of the 1860s, this pair of well-carved pine torchère stands represent a decadent court jester drawn from a character in a popular nineteenth-century romantic legend or theatrical comedy. Gingerly posed on a circular base, clad in breeches and a coat which cling to his sumptuously molded body, he wears a cap and slippers hung with bells. His mischievous grin attests to his devious intentions.

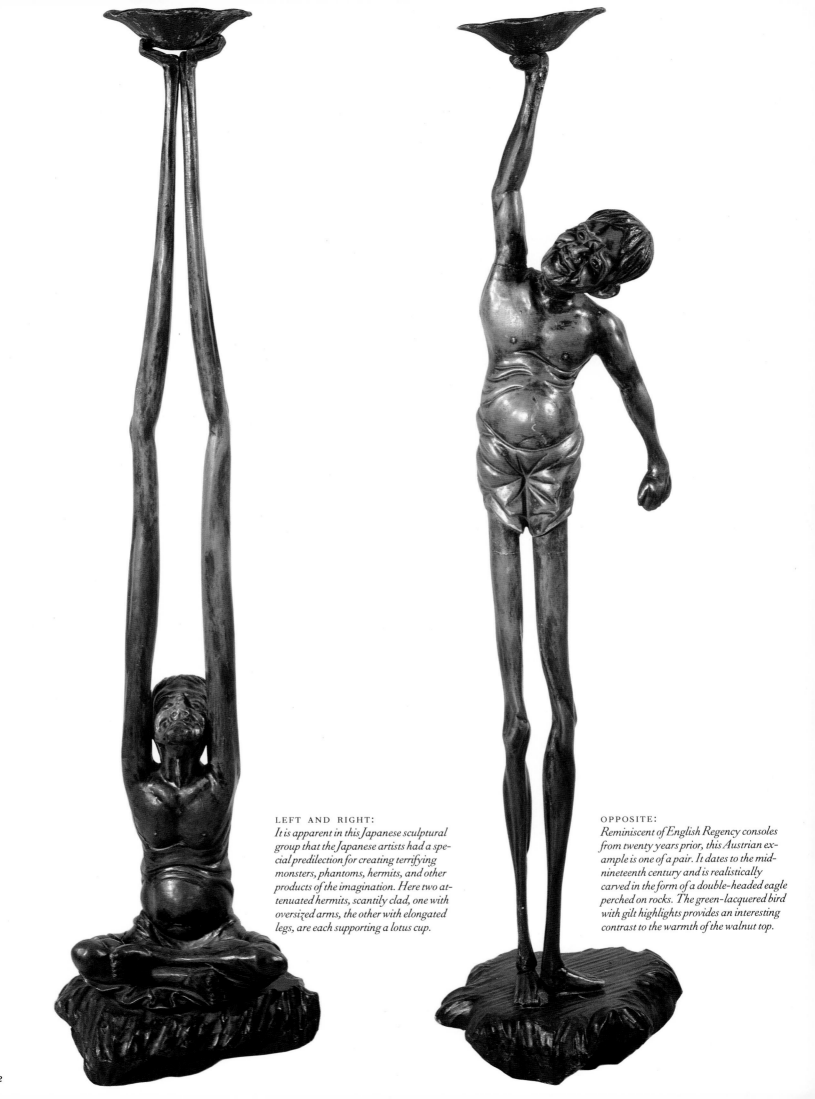

LEFT AND RIGHT:
It is apparent in this Japanese sculptural group that the Japanese artists had a special predilection for creating terrifying monsters, phantoms, hermits, and other products of the imagination. Here two attenuated hermits, scantily clad, one with oversized arms, the other with elongated legs, are each supporting a lotus cup.

OPPOSITE:
Reminiscent of English Regency consoles from twenty years prior, this Austrian example is one of a pair. It dates to the mid-nineteenth century and is realistically carved in the form of a double-headed eagle perched on rocks. The green-lacquered bird with gilt highlights provides an interesting contrast to the warmth of the walnut top.

RIGHT:

Teapots were purchased by everyone in England during the nineteenth century. It was therefore understandable that they would be an object subject to imaginative designs. This unusual pair is modeled in the form of monkeys seated upon a stump. Their upward-turned tails form the handles, with a snake apparently caught between their legs modeled to form the spout. The humorous effect is heightened by grins and feathered conical caps. They date to the second half of the nineteenth century and are made from multicolored creamware-glazed earthenware.

RIGHT:

Cast-iron door stops were extremely popular during the late nineteenth and early twentieth centuries. These two, which retain their original paint, are cast in the form of Punch and Judy.

OPPOSITE AND ABOVE:

This Venetian painted and parcel-gilt figural pedestal dates from the third quarter of the eighteenth century. A whimsically carved winged satyr sitting atop a leafy stump supports a foliate-scrolled cornucopia, which probably held a fern- or fruit-filled bowl.

RIGHT:

The hydra, a three-headed mythological beast slain by Hercules, provides the theme for this pair of French nineteenth-century sculptural three-light bronze candelabrum.

RIGHT:

Made in France during the 1920s, these art deco porcelain wall appliqués are highly stylized and modeled in the form of a clown and clowness.

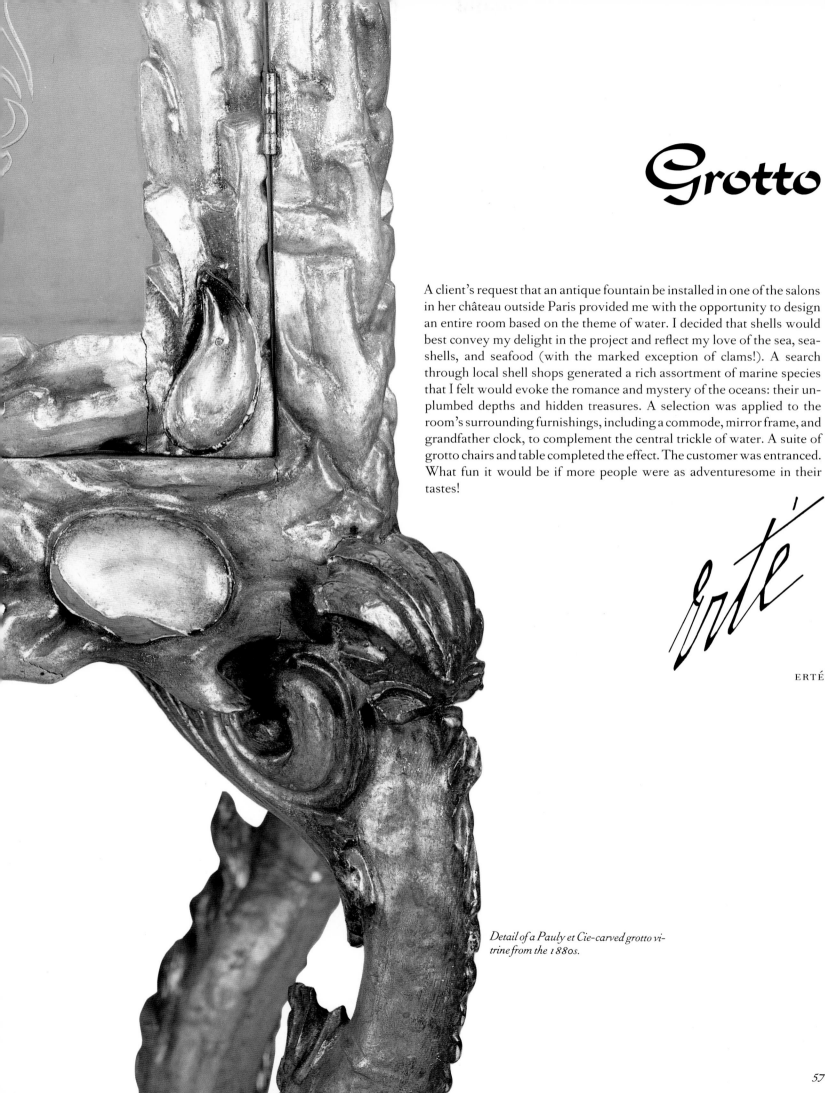

Grotto

A client's request that an antique fountain be installed in one of the salons in her château outside Paris provided me with the opportunity to design an entire room based on the theme of water. I decided that shells would best convey my delight in the project and reflect my love of the sea, seashells, and seafood (with the marked exception of clams!). A search through local shell shops generated a rich assortment of marine species that I felt would evoke the romance and mystery of the oceans: their unplumbed depths and hidden treasures. A selection was applied to the room's surrounding furnishings, including a commode, mirror frame, and grandfather clock, to complement the central trickle of water. A suite of grotto chairs and table completed the effect. The customer was entranced. What fun it would be if more people were as adventuresome in their tastes!

Erté

ERTÉ

Detail of a Pauly et Cie-carved grotto vitrine from the 1880s.

This extremely rare nautical carved vitrine, attributed to the Italian firm of Pauly et Cie, may be one of a handful surviving from the 1880s. The rectangular case is carved to resemble pieces of coral adorned with nautilus shells, mollusks, starfish, and sea snakes. The whole is raised on eel-form supports joined by a platform stretcher ending in shell-carved scrolled feet. The silvered finish is highlighted in tones of blue, red, and brown.

From the birth of the nubile Aphrodite, goddess of love and fertility, whom it delivered from the ocean to the Greek civilization of antiquity, the shell has always captured man's sense of the romantic and exotic. During the Middle Ages, after its initial spiritual and sexual symbolism had evolved into an aesthetic one, the shell continued to captivate Europe's wealthy. As navigation expanded man's horizons in the fifteenth and sixteenth centuries, it increased his knowledge of foreign shells. Among the cargoes of exotica returning from the New Worlds—especially to Amsterdam from Holland's new colonies in the East Indies—was a treasure trove of tropical shells. The science of conchology became a separate study within the broader field of marine biology.

Renaissance and Mannerist gold- and silversmiths created lavish virtuoso objects inspired by the shell: Triton-wielding putti straddled gold-mounted nautilus cups raised on sculpted turtle bases, and four-square rigged galleons, or *nefs,* in which a shell formed the hull of a vessel mounted in parcel-gilt silver, were exquisitely rendered for a princely patronage. Scalloped snuff boxes were similarly commissioned. In other disciplines, the shell established itself equally as a dominant decorative theme: in Italian majolica (Capo di Monte), German porcelain (Kandler, for Meissen), English and Irish porcelain (Bow, Chelsea, Worcester, Derby, Coalport, and Belleek), and Dutch ceramics (Delft, Rotterdam, and Utrecht), it was repeatedly preferred for important commissions.

In the eighteenth century the shell's status as a royal ornament was secured by its popularity at the courts of Louis XIV and XV. The rococo style, derived from the French word *rocaille,* which described a rock-and-shell form of decoration, became the Bourbon court's most popular form of embellishment. *Ebénistes* joined their counterparts in other disciplines with the application to their furniture of a fanciful array of veneered and ormolu shell-form motifs. Architecture kept apace. The façade of the celebrated House of the Shells in Salamanca, Spain, built as a palace for Dr. D. Rodrigo Arias Maldonado circa 1512, was adorned with rows of scalloped shells. A later manifestation of the shell's architectural allure was the Tempietto in Rome, the forerunner of St. Peter's, which Bramante decorated throughout with scallop-shaped niches and fountains.

The shell's myriad shapes, patterns, and colors—there are roughly 100,000 species of mollusks, including snails, mussels, and cephalopods—conjured up images of mystical foreign lands and uncharted oceans that fascinated Europe at the time even more than today, though the impulse to pick a shell up while strolling at water's edge remains irresistible.

In the eighteenth century the aristocracy in England and Europe were caught up in a craze for folly building—the erection of pavilions, pagodas, and grottoes—to the point that no gentleman's estate could be considered complete without at least one such indulgence. A duke, for example, might even have one of each. To have no eccentricity became, in itself, an eccentricity. These follies, all gay and richly embellished, were found primarily in England, France, and Italy. One noteworthy example was the scintillating shell pavilion at Goodwood Park, Sussex, dating to the mid-

1700s. Today, surviving examples of these isolated fantasies are imbued with the melancholy charm of neglect.

Garden and indoor grottoes were designed as subterranean caves or caverns in which the presence of water, actual or implied, was a prerequisite. Artificial stalactites and waterfalls provided a natural ambience, as did shells applied as mural ornaments or strewn around the floor's perimeter.

The search for a complementary furniture style with which to decorate grottoes no doubt provided the stimulus for the furniture shown in these pages. When and where the style evolved, however, has long confounded historians. This is rather curious, given the fact that several European museums have acquired examples of such furniture, many recently. In Germany, for example, the Nationalgalerie in Berlin purchased a grotto *guéridon* through the local trade in 1957; four years later the Kunstgewerbemuseum made a similar purchase from a dealer of a table. In Vienna, the Osterreichisches Museum für angewandte Kunst acquired a third example in 1973. The three are so similar in style and execution that it is safe to suggest that they were manufactured by the same cabinetry shop. A fourth example, donated to the Victoria and Albert Museum in 1934, is closely related stylistically, although it includes a more intricately carved top and sea-horse feet. Similar comparisons become evident when one examines grotto chairs in European museum collections. Two examples in the Muzeum Narodowe w Warszawie in Warsaw—an armchair with openwork dolphin arms and a matching side chair—incorporate bold C-scrolled backs fashioned as scallop shells. The Schloss Köpenick Kunstgewerbemuseum in East Berlin and the Bayerisches Nationalmuseum in Munich contain similar armchairs, which vary only in the placement of ornamental sea-horse heads at the foot of their backrests. A settee for two—termed a *confident*—with an S-formed serpentine frame enclosing reversing seats, which sold at the Hotel Drouot in Paris in 1982, is comprised of the same components, although its shell backs are more formal than the dynamic and asymmetrical forms of the models discussed above.

Grotto furniture is comprised of four basic components: scalloped shells, sea horses, dolphins, and triton horns. Combinations vary. Whereas, for example, most models incorporate legs carved as triton-horn shells, these are, on occasion, replaced by sea horses or dolphins. Small stylistic changes are also evident: The sea horses on some models are rendered more as menacing sea dragons or even as real horses, while applied crabs, starfish, mussels, and conch shells add definition to some of the more ambitious models. Despite such variables, however, there is a general stylistic uniformity that argues that grotto furniture was conceived and manufactured within a small community of workshops.

For many years this type of grotto furniture was presumed to be of eighteenth-century origin, in part, no doubt, because prototypes from the mid-1700s drew on a similar, although restrained, range of shell motifs. Chippendale was among the first to design a grotto chair, which was illustrated in the third edition of his 1762 Directory in the section on "Garden Seats" (plate 24). It is questionable, however, whether the model, which

ABOVE:
As early as the late seventeenth century, Italian artisans incorporated nautical creatures in their designs for pianos and dressing stools. In this unique nineteenth-century silver-gilt grotto example, the shell-form seat is raised on a tripod base carved with stylized sea serpents. It is attributed to the firm of Remi & Ci of Venice.

OPPOSITE:
This Venetian tripod jewelry casket, attributed to Pauly et Cie, Venice, is decorated with shells and sea horses and is unusual, as most grotto-inspired furniture takes the form of seat furniture.

included a seat and back designed as an open scallop raised on carved dolphin feet, was ever executed. Another eighteenth-century example, now in the Victoria and Albert Museum and originally from Woodhall Park, Hertford, is comprised of shells, snails, and crustaceans. Another chair in the Victoria and Albert collection, thought to have been designed by Francis Cleyn for the garden at Holland House, has a *sgabello*-type form enhanced with a crested scallop back. At Petworth there are several similar examples painted in black and gold. Other eighteenth-century models, both in England and on the Continent, contain carved marine motifs applied to traditional chair forms for use in country houses and grotto rooms, like the one at Woburn Abbey. All of these, however, are of conventional form with restrained ornamentation and are far removed in spirit from the rococo exuberance of the models under discussion and illustrated in this chapter.

Despite the relatively large volume of grotto furniture that has appeared in the marketplace from year to year, both in Europe and the United States, its identity has remained elusive, perplexing both curators and collectors. A small table in the Berlin Kunstgewerbemuseum, for example, supported on triton-horn feet beneath a column entwined by a sea horse, was catalogued as "Austrian, second quarter of eighteenth century." A similar suite of seat furniture in the Germanisches Nationalmuseum in Nuremberg, dated in its literature to about 1730, was described as "unusual," its origin given as a "grotto room" in a Saxon castle, and its creators thought to be rather "temperamental." The Bayerisches Nationalmuseum considered this type of furniture as "beyond all borders of taste," while in Berlin it was generally considered to have been created by a "wandering troupe of Italian carvers who once came to the North and worked in Bohemian castles and Saxon noble houses." In another erroneous attribution, Heinrich Kreisel identified it as Franconian, from 1760–70.

Careful examination of a grotto piece of furniture, however, repudiates any attempt to link it to the eighteenth century. Its construction is conceived and executed in a rudimentary and often unsteady manner that is contrary to the rich traditions of eighteenth-century cabinetry. Its components are not joined in the conventional manner to which even the most adventurous furniture of the period conformed. Wooden pegs are absent; in their place are commercial screws that secure the backrest to the seat and the latter to the legs. The recessed placement of the screws and their concealment beneath the piece's gessoed finish prove that they are original to it. To compensate for the absence of doweling, reinforcing struts have often been applied to the undersides of seats and tabletops. Further examination reveals that the structural components were finished by machine, rather than manually. Finally, both the quality of the wood employed and that of the carving are primitive compared to the standards set by eighteenth-century joiners.

A final argument against an eighteenth-century origin for grotto furniture is that two of its standard models—the confident and the rocking chair—were invented after 1800. Whereas one could conceivably argue that they were later additions to an existing grotto line, this is highly im-

This Venetian rocking chair, manufactured in the 1890s by the firm Pauly et Cie, is overlaid with silver gilt and carved to simulate shells with stylized dolphin and dragon supports.

probable. The rocking chair, for example, made its appearance in the 1840s, primarily in the United States, as a form of children's furniture. Published for the first time in the 1845 *Encyclopedia of Domestic Economy,* the model was shown at the 1851 Crystal Palace exhibition, while Thonet's first rocking chair dates to 1869. The S-shaped confident, more widely known as a tête-à-tête, was also a mid-nineteenth-century creation, making its debut circa 1840. An example, manufactured by the upholsterers Jeanselme *frères,* was illustrated at the time in Pasquier's "Cahiers de Dessins d'Ameublement." Another example, pictured in Wilhelm Kembel's journal for carpenters and wallpaperers, was later popularized in the United Kingdom and the United States.

Most grotto furniture is finished in a lacquered silver leaf heightened with an overlay of metallic brownish giltglaze that provides definition to the fluting on the scallops and other carved decorative details. The silver's iridescence effectively simulates the nacreous secretions that form on the interior of abalones and clams. On occasion, an isolated shell is highlighted in another color.

Where and when, then, did grotto furniture originate, and who were its creators? The trail leads appropriately to Venice, a city born of the water and with a rich heritage of nautical odysseys. There, a Signor Pauly appears to have begun to manufacture it in the late 1880s. Little is known of Pauly beyond that he was born in 1866 and that his firm manufactured the grotto line until the 1930s, catering initially to a clientele who used it to furnish their winter gardens, which were in high fashion in the late Victorian era. Occasional pieces bear the identification *Pauly et Cie, Venise, Ponte Consorʒi, Fabrique de Meubles et Verreries Artistiques.* Another Venetian manufacturer of grotto furniture was Remi, who signed his pieces with a metal tag, *Remi & Ci* (sic), *Fabrique de Meubles Verreries Marbre Mosaiques.*

Grotto furniture is today enjoying one of its intermittent revivals in popularity, the last one having occurred in the early 1930s, when Helena Rubenstein selected examples with which to redecorate her chic Parisian apartment. Grotto furniture's allure has also drawn the politicians Franz Jonas and Indira Gandhi and the artists Henri Matisse, Otto Dix, and Hans Koernig. It remains an eccentric and endearing style that tempts the viewer with thoughts of exotic lands and cultures.

LEFT:
This tripod plant stand with a typical shell-carved top rests on a branchlike support, with an exotic dragon above legs carved in the form of sea horses atop shells.

This nautical chair is somewhat unconventional in that an open back is formed by a serpentlike fish, which continues to form the arms. The splat takes the form of a wave terminating in a sea horse's head. The seat and legs are similar to those on other Italian grotto chairs.

65

PRECEDING PAGES:
Three late-nineteenth-century Italian shell-carved silver-gilt grottoesque armchairs and a center table were chosen by Erté to complement the shell-mounted commodes, mirrors, and tall case clock he designed for the foyer of the salle à manger *in the Château du Sorcier.*

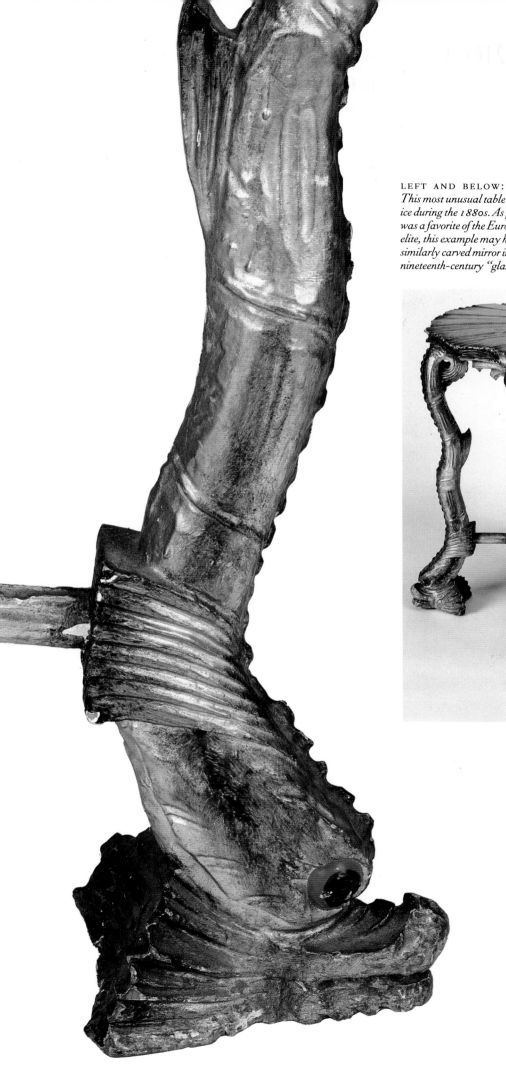

LEFT AND BELOW:
This most unusual table was made in Venice during the 1880s. As grotto furniture was a favorite of the European nouveau elite, this example may have sat beneath a similarly carved mirror in the home of a nineteenth-century "glamor girl."

OVERLEAF:
This silver-gilt armchair dates to the late nineteenth century. The crescent-shaped shell-carved backs terminate in a stylized sea horse flanked by fish-form arms. The scalloped plank seats rest on scrolled supports resembling oyster shells, which surround pearl-like cabochons.

OVERLEAF, P. 71:
Although tête-à-têtes were a common form of seat furniture during the latter part of the nineteenth century, grotto examples are rare.

LEFT:
The double-chair-back, late-nineteenth-century love seat shown here continues the mid-eighteenth-century Venetian tradition of adopting familiar aquatic species to form whimsical furnishings.

OVERLEAF:
Triple-chair-back settees with contoured seats are a rarity among Venetian grotto furnishings. In this "silvered" example, three large shells form the back and seat, interspersed with smaller shells. It was manufactured in the late nineteenth century by Pauly et Cie, Venice. The trestle supports incorporate winged sea horses joined by a driftwood stretcher centering a shell.

OVERLEAF, P. 75:
Following the baroque tradition, three shells form the top of this nineteenth-century grottoesque center table. They rest on a pair of dragonlike serpents with feathered tails, which are joined by a stretcher carved with another exotic dragon.

TOP:
A variety of mollusks, crabs, fish, and coral adorn the surround on this early-twentieth-century Italian grotto work of art. One could go as far as to use the caption Le Fruti di Mare *to describe this polychrome-tinted silver-gilt mirror, attributed to Pauly et Cie, Venice.*

ABOVE AND LEFT:
The shell-carved top of this nineteenth-century Venetian grotto side table is raised on supports carved to resemble driftwood, entwined with sea serpents and highlighted with shells.

ABOVE:
This turquoise-glazed majolica jardiniere in the form of a nautilus shell is the perfect pot for an overgrown, dew-laden fern.

BELOW:
A Scallop-shell back detail characterizes this rare grotto tête-à-tête.

Horn & Antler

I was introduced to horn and antler furniture in the early 1950s in a small Manhattan restaurant, the Hapsburg, which was operated by my good friend, Ludwig Bemelmans. He had little money, so he decorated his dining room with a buffet made from antlers, above which he painted a trompe l'oeil mirror framed in antlers. This excited my interest in the use of horns and antlers in furniture and led me to investigate the origins of this exotic style of decoration. Here is what I found:

Hunting wild animals was man's vocation from the beginning of human civilization. He celebrated his achievements by portraying the joys of the chase on the stone walls of the caves he inhabited, and later in history, on the hides of the animals he had slain. Even after animals were domesticated and the necessity for hunting was eliminated, man still retained the joy and excitement of the hunt, leading to the transformation of his vocation into a compelling avocation.

It is no surprise, then, that horns and antlers, which were impervious to the ravages of time, were retained as trophies of the chase and were eventually used in the fifteenth and sixteenth centuries to decorate chandeliers and finally, in the eighteenth century, to become components of chairs, tables, and other pieces of furniture.

It took thousands of years for a vocation to become an avocation and only five hundred years for trophies of the hunt to be memorialized into objects of decor and utility.

STANLEY MARCUS

OPPOSITE:
A stag's head decorates the base of a whimsical piece of antler furniture.

From time immemorial, trophies of the chase have been used to decorate the log cabins and hunting lodges from which hunters and sportsmen sally forth to bag their kill. Walls replete with mounted antlers and stuffed animal heads identify these traditional male preserves, where the idea to fashion horns into furniture was probably first conceived. By the fifteenth century they were used as crude storage racks, coat hooks, and chandeliers. In a comprehensive article on the derivation of such furniture in a 1977 Victoria and Albert Museum publication, Simon Jervis noted that the earliest recorded usage of antlers as ornamentation was on Gothic *Kronleuchters,* or circular chandeliers. Comprised of a circular steel ring set with candle prickets, these chandeliers were mounted with pairs of antlers joined at the base by a carved and polychromed head of the Virgin. One example, in the Stadtischesmuseum in Erfurt, dates to circa 1400. Variations included the figure of Saint Ursula, such as that found in a model in the *Rathaus* at Luneberg, Saint Paul, or Christ. Later examples, termed *Leuchterweibchen,* dispensed with the ring and incorporated the torso of a bare-breasted maiden who appeared to hover above the room's occupants on antler wings. Early examples of these chandeliers were illustrated in a manuscript by Willem Vrelant in the university library at Erlanger and in engravings by Lucas Cranach, circa 1540.

During the Renaissance, *Leuchterweibchen* were less rigidly ecclesiastical. An example designed by Dürer in 1513 incorporated a mermaid, while others by the same artist, published by W. C. Fleischmann of Nuremberg, included a dragon and a cupid with bow. Chandeliers of this type, incorporating a mix of elk, reindeer, and moose antlers, remained in vogue until the mid-1600s, when their popularity waned. Revived interest came in the early nineteenth century, particularly in northern Europe, where furniture manufacturers introduced a revised version of the *Leuchterweibchen.* The earlier carved wood torsos were now often omitted, providing fixtures with a lighter and more symmetrical appeal.

Although occasional evidence of horn seat furniture is recorded throughout the Middle Ages, its use only became widespread around 1800. Sheraton's *Cabinet Dictionary* of 1803 showed an adjustable hunting chair whose legs were fashioned from single antlers. It was described as "a temporary resting place for one that is fatigued, as hunters generally are." By 1820 the cabinetmaking shop of Josef Danhauser, in existence from 1804 to 1838, had developed the concept fully for commercial purposes. Examples in the firm's drawings, now in the Osterreichisches Museum für angewandte Kunst in Vienna, reveal a wide selection of models. A sofa, for example, was ornamented with stuffed stag's heads and antlers. Judging from their romantic interpretation, these sketches probably date to the 1830s, when Danhauser had been succeeded by his son, also named Josef.

Horn furniture remained a regional curiosity until the 1851 Crystal Palace Exhibition in London, when the Victorian fascination with bizarre forms and materials won it a wider audience. Its primary producer was H. F. C. Rampendahl of Hamburg, whose "various specimens of staghorn furniture," comprising a writing-bureau, candelabra, chairs, sofa,

BELOW:
This humorous twentieth-century antler and antler-veneered console table is probably copied from a nineteenth-century Bavarian design. The profusion of antlers that form the base center a stag's head, conjuring the image of a deer peering through the forest.

and table, were illustrated in the Exhibition's official catalogue. Unlike the other items, the writing-bureau was not constructed of horns but was designed as a conventional fall-front desk decorated on the front with a carved miniature stag's head and stag medallions flanked by arrangements of horns on the column capitals and sides. Completing this strange composition on the top was a gazebo within a pair of flaring antlers. Rampendahl's display was said to have met with the "unanimous approval of the British, Scottish, and Irish nobility and gentry." A suite of furniture in the Horn Room at Osborne House on the Isle of Wight, which no doubt reminded Prince Albert of his German upbringing when he and Queen Victoria visited their island retreat, is so similar to Rampendahl's 1851 exhibit that it can safely be attributed to him.

Attempts at novelty punctuated the mid-1800s, many monstrously ugly. The giant chandelier displayed by W. Jaehnert of Berlin at the 1867 Exposition in Paris, for example, featured a mix of antlers, horns, teeth, and hooves that its manufacturer boasted took twelve years to complete. Other models likewise overstepped convention and the limits of good taste as designers grappled with how to insert candle holders and human and animal forms into the bristling configuration of branched antlers that characterized horn light fixtures. Later examples, adapted for gas and electricity, were equally heavy-handed.

By 1862, when Rampendahl showed a further selection of horn furniture at the London Exhibition, the trade in this type of furnishings had established itself in Frankfurt-am-Main. The most celebrated example of its use was at the Platte, the hunting lodge of the dukes of Nassau, near Wiesbaden, built between 1822 and 1824 and destroyed during World War II. Another noted installation, for a hunting box at Ohrade, near Hluboka in Czechoslovakia, included chairs, a table covered with deerskin, and a large deerskin carpet, all attributed to Martin Klenovic, a forester in the service of Prince Schwarzenberg. Wounded by a poacher as a young man, Klenovic spent his retirement from 1849 to 1885 in the manufacture of horn pieces.

Another participant at the 1862 London Exhibition was R. Friedrich Böhler, who was awarded a silver medal for his display of stag-horn furnishings. Situated in Frankfurt, Böhler advertised regularly at the time in Murray's *Handbook to Southern Germany*, published in England. He produced a wide selection of horn accessories, in-

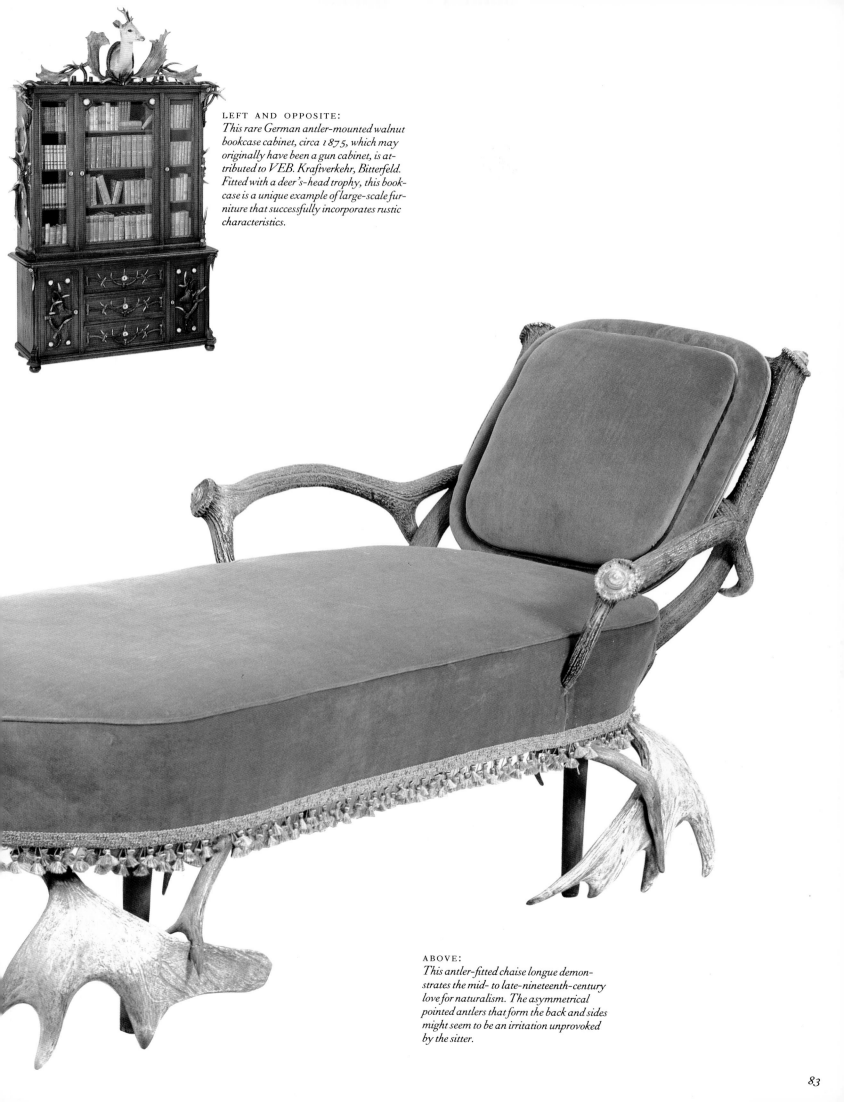

LEFT AND OPPOSITE:
This rare German antler-mounted walnut bookcase cabinet, circa 1875, which may originally have been a gun cabinet, is attributed to VEB. Kraftverkehr, Bitterfeld. Fitted with a deer's-head trophy, this bookcase is a unique example of large-scale furniture that successfully incorporates rustic characteristics.

ABOVE:
This antler-fitted chaise longue demonstrates the mid- to late-nineteenth-century love for naturalism. The asymmetrical pointed antlers that form the back and sides might seem to be an irritation unprovoked by the sitter.

83

ABOVE:
This late-nineteenth-century English brass-mounted walnut and antler jardiniere is one of the few examples of trophy furniture attributable to the firm Barry & Co., Bradford.

cluding pen holders, knife handles, riding whips, pipes, and "sofa-rugs or foot-cloths of skins of wild animals with heads preserved." Böhler's London agent was listed as Messrs. J. & R. McCracken.

Further examples of European horn furniture were displayed at the 1876 Philadelphia Exhibition, including, in the related field of taxidermy, a bizarre stuffed bear designed as a dumbwaiter, offered by the firm of naturalists, Ward & Company. The following year Messrs. Jetley of North Audley Street, London, displayed furniture made of horns from the sambar deer and Indian antelope. Included was a suite for an Indian nabob.

Labels found on examples of horn and antler furniture identify other European makers: in Germany, the firms of Kraftverkehr of Bitterfeld, C. W. Fleischmann of Nuremberg, and H. F. C. Rampendahl of Hamburg; in Sweden, the firm of Fortardiget Av Gulddragare Manne Bjork in Nacka; in Austria, E. N. Keitel of Vienna; and in England, J. Parker of Woodstock.

THE UNITED STATES

In the United States, horn furniture became the preserve of one manufacturer, Wenzel Friedrich (1827–1902), who emigrated from his native Bohemia to Texas in 1853. Arriving in Indianola, Texas, Friedrich traveled by oxen train to San Antonio, at the time a small trading post on the outskirts of civilization, for which the Alamo was still a recent memory. Tiring quickly of his initial employment in the grocery business, Friedrich reverted to his Austrian training as a cabinetmaker. In 1880 he added horn furniture to his existing line of revival styles. Nine years later the firm's thirty-two page catalogue boasted a wide selection of horn models, including an "extra large" easy chair, "perfect" rockers, office chairs, ottomans, music stools, and flower stands. A hall stand, listed as an "improved hat-rack," was billed as the firm's pièce de résistance. Comprised of thirty-two horns applied to a horn-veneered frame, the piece was priced at a hefty $250.

No doubt conversant from his upbringing with the demand for antler furniture in Europe, Friedrich found the American equivalent in the Texas longhorn steer. Between 1860 and 1880 giant herds of these steer were driven from the Lone Star State up dusty cattle trails to railheads in Kansas cowtowns such as Wichita, Dodge City, and Abilene—perilous journeys through Indian territories now deeply woven into the fabric of America's legendary Wild West and its cowboy legacy.

Initially, longhorn cattle were in plentiful supply, enabling Friedrich to purchase a large inventory of horns from local San Antonio stockyards at $5 per pair. These he sorted into sizes. For armchairs, at least three sets were necessary; one pair, the largest, to form the arms, and the other two to serve as the framework for the chair's back. Additional pairs were added for deluxe models, their protruding sharp ends capped with acorn finials to prevent flesh wounds and impaled clothing. Highly complex models, such as a sofa embellished with forty-two horns arranged symmetrically in pairs, appear to today's uninitiated viewer as prickly instruments of torture!

A Bavarian antler, oak, and horn smoking
stand, circa 1875, this piece is fitted with a
pipe stand, three variously sized horn cups,
and a tray, all sitting atop a ledge raised on
a group of entwined antlers.

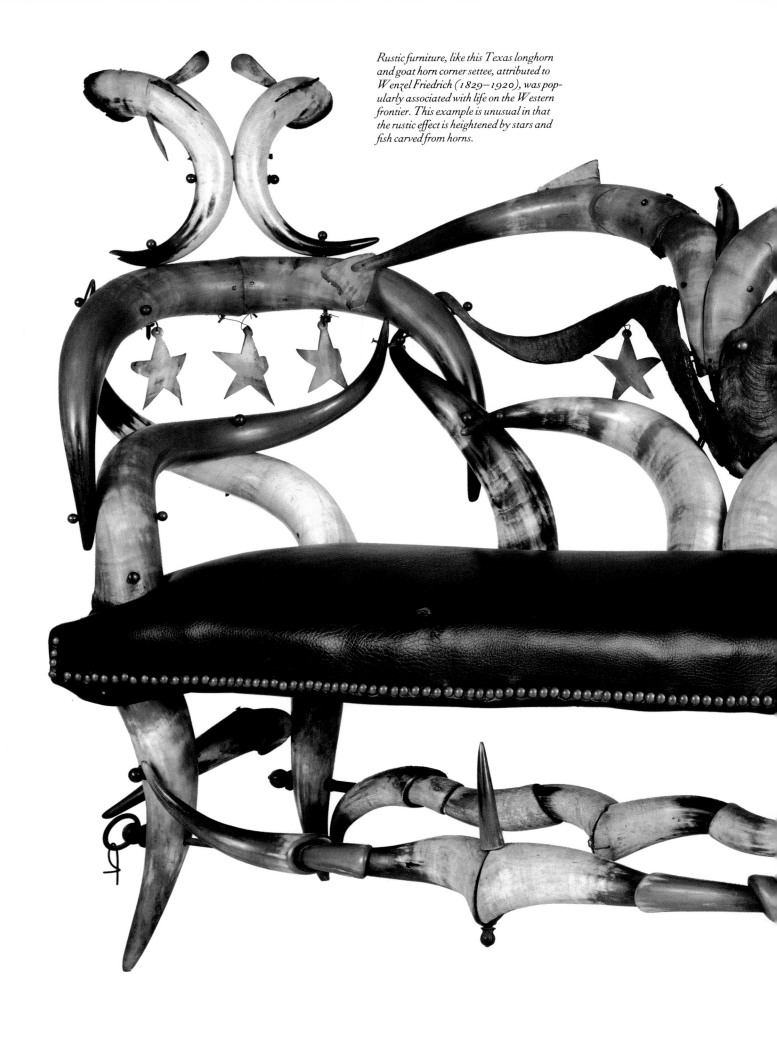

Rustic furniture, like this Texas longhorn and goat horn corner settee, attributed to Wenzel Friedrich (1829–1920), was popularly associated with life on the Western frontier. This example is unusual in that the rustic effect is heightened by stars and fish carved from horns.

On selecting his horns, Friedrich placed them in large vats of boiling water to soften their rough outer surfaces, which were then pared away with a blade. After cleaning, they were dried in sunlight and then vigorously buffed with a cloth to obtain a high surface sheen. The exaggerated curves and angles found on some horns were achieved by immersing them in boiling water until they were soft and pliable.

During this process, the chair's wooden seat was assembled in preparation for the polished horns to be fitted. Each of these was first filled with plaster of Paris to provide strength and then sealed at the mouth with circular wooden blocks, before being attached to the chair's frame with large wooden screws. Upholstery ranged from cowhide and Angora goatskin to plush silk, fox, catamount (an American lynx) and—the most sumptuous—jaguar, which commanded an additional $2 to $5. An enterprising decorative fillip was provided by the application of gold Favrile glass castors, which Friedrich commissioned from Tiffany Studios in New York. For his signature, he chose the Texas Star, carved in ivory.

Friedrich realized that horns are comprised of layers of protein, like fingernails, separated by thin films of natural oil. Prolonged boiling produced thin sheets of horn which could be pressed flat and dried and then cut into desired shapes for attachment by glue to the furniture's wooden frame. Eye-catching veneers were produced in this manner for tabletops and seat aprons.

Friedrich's endeavors were greeted with enthusiasm and garnered him much prestige, including numerous gold-medal awards at shows such as the New Orleans Industrial & Cotton Centennial Exposition, in 1884–85 and the Southern Exposition in Louisville, Kentucky, in 1886. His overseas clientele included such royal patronage as Queen Victoria, Bismarck, Kaiser Wilhelm I, and the president of France. Nearer home, however, he could boast of a far less celebrated kind of customer; for the most part, owners of bordellos or saloons in the confederacy of old Southern states.

Longhorns lasted barely a decade, being replaced in the early 1890s by a short-horned breed, called *fat stock*. The demand for longhorns was reduced to a trickle, particularly after the railroad reached Texas. Friedrich had to turn to Mexico to replenish his inventory.

The Victorian homeowner found horn-and-antler furniture quaint and romantic, as we do today. Its basic call to nature helped him to hold the encroaching industrial revolution at bay. And if he preferred not to consider that it was a hunting trophy of sorts, he could distance himself from this fact in the realization that most mid-1800s examples were comprised of a mix of indigenous and foreign species of horn and not from a single animal, which somehow seemed crueler.

OPPOSITE:
Hung from the ceiling of a great hall, this nineteenth-century Bavarian twelve-light chandelier differs from most, as it incorporates both stag and steer horns.

LEFT:
This antler and ivory two-light wall sconce dates from 1860 to 1890. It may have been made in the British Isles. The shaped backplate contains two pairs of small antler points, which surround an antler and a plaque carved with two bucks. The curved arms are shaped from a wire armature fitted with antler segments, and the circular ivory drip pan and candle nozzles are capped with antler veneers.

BELOW, LEFT AND RIGHT:
Candle stands of this type would have been used on a desk in a study adorned with other rustic or horn-made furnishings. In these examples, antler points support the candle nozzles.

ABOVE:
A probable exhibition item, this standish contains a pair of twisted mountain-goat horns supporting a glass bottle.

RIGHT:
Intended to be used in a dining room amid other horn-decorated rustic furniture, this mid- to late-nineteenth-century cellarette of serpentine form, fitted with antlers, is similar to hundreds of cellarettes created in the nineteenth century.

PRECEDING PAGES:
An antler recamier, fauteuil, and chande-lier are among the furnishings in the Grand Salon of the Château du Sorcier. The early-sixteenth-century fireplace provides a rustic foil for Erté's selection of horn furniture.

BELOW:
This Victorian-inspired Texas steerhorn settee from the early part of the twentieth century is fitted with nineteen pairs of well-matched horns and eight single horns posi-tioned to form a double-chair-back settee, surmounted by crescents. Trophy furniture of this type was a favorite of Theodore Roosevelt.

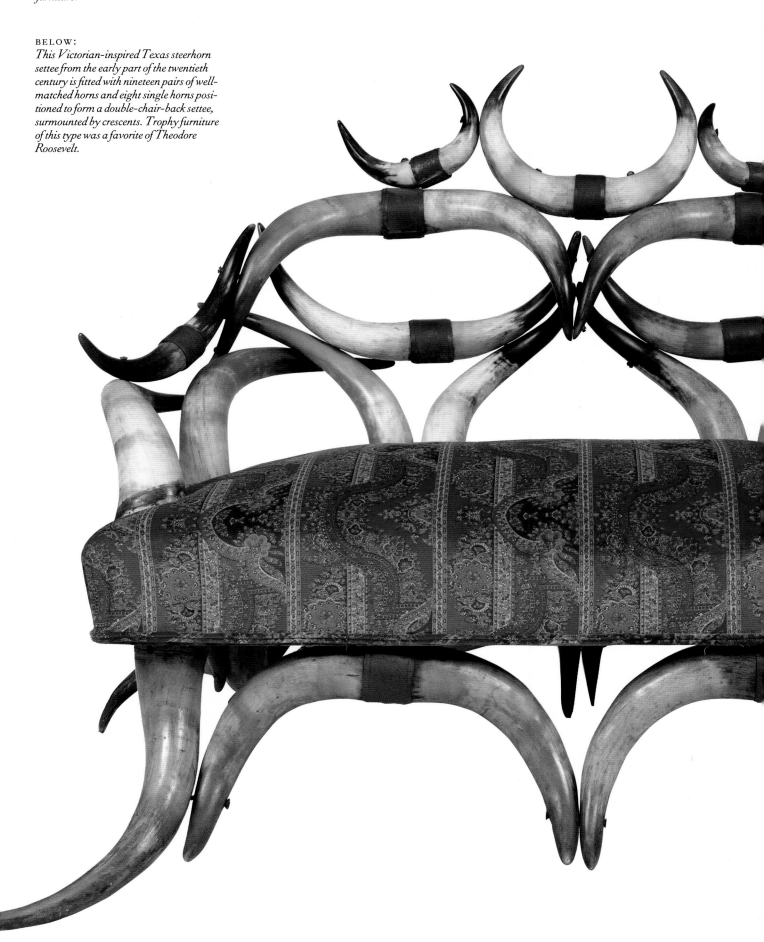

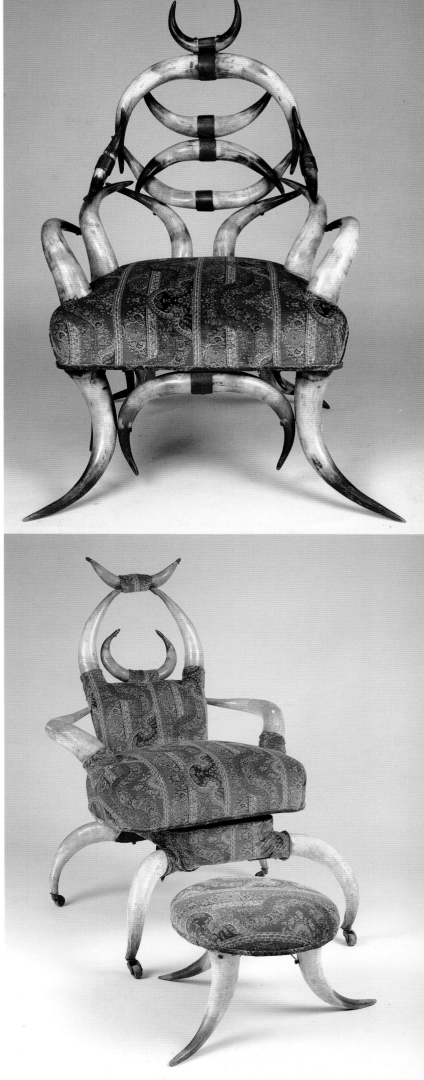

RIGHT:
This Texas steerhorn armchair is typical of many trophy armchairs used in billiard rooms, smoking dens, and summer camps.

BELOW RIGHT:
This American paisley-upholstered steerhorn swiveling armchair with matching upholstered stool could have been made in Texas, Kansas, or Oklahoma and may have graced a New York dandy's smoke-filled den.

This Austrian staghorn, antler, and oak side chair dates to the third quarter of the nineteenth century and is of great interest, as it bears the manufacturer's label: E. N. Keitel, Wien. *Its back is symmetrically formed by a pair of crossed antlers, with a seat raised on three crossed antlers. The overall decorative effect is intensified by the* faux *leopard upholstered back and seat.*

With its upholstered padded back and headrest, this steerhorn armchair, circa 1900, would appear to be more comfortable than most.

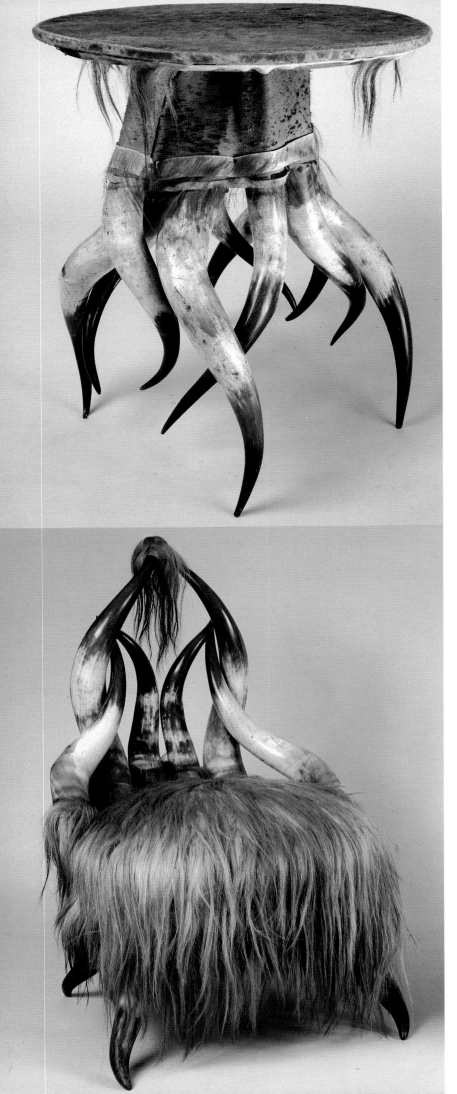

LEFT:
This well-proportioned hide-covered horn occasional table is American and dates from the early part of the twentieth century.

LEFT AND OPPOSITE:
A twentieth-century American steerhorn trophy chair, this might be a souvenir of an Everest expedition.

OPPOSITE:
*An amusing spiderlike steerhorn chair, this
piece consists of horns surrounding an elongated padded back surmounted by a hoof.
The oval seat is raised on thirteen horns of
various sizes.*

ABOVE:
*This English staghorn center table, circa
1890, has a circular top fitted with a re-
poussé-decorated copper sheet chased with
strapwork and stylized crescents, reminiscent of Celtic designs. It is raised on an
hourglass support which is formed by
antlers.*

ABOVE:
*This mid- to late-nineteenth-century um-
brella stand, attributed to J. Parker,
Woodstock, is made from eleven well-
matched velvetlike antlers affixed to a circular turned oak support with carved
hooved feet. It may have been purchased as
a souvenir from an exhibition or a
catalogue.*

Designed to accent the interior of a European country retreat, this pair of rustic staghorn-mounted side chairs date to the third quarter of the nineteenth century. The backs are fitted with two pairs of matched antlers, which form the chair surround and central splat. The seats are also fitted with antler points and raised on antler supports.

This pedestal desk, attributed to Kraftver-kehr, is fitted with antlers and adorned with carved rabbits' heads. This desk was probably part of the furnishings of a hunting lodge or sportsman's study.

"Black Forest"

For a one-time curator, an antiques buff who spends his days writing and talking art history, the Black Forest looms large as a picturesque region of beautiful forests dotted with impressive structures that combine the timely Gothic and the timeless rustic. The architecture of this area is not easy to explain in basic stylistic terms, so it is no surprise to find that the furniture called by the name of the region is whimsical. The best-known efforts are made of rough unfinished wood that looks unhewn but is embellished with carved details of animals that show the craftsmen were skillful yet knowing and intentionally simple in their designs. A scholar might remember that such furniture, without the carved animal detail, is to be found in seventeenth-century Dutch paintings by artists like Teniers or Ostade. Similar garden furniture appears in some eighteenth-century design books but without the animal detail.

The furniture associated with the Black Forest is a delightful and perfect expression of the late nineteenth century. Depending upon traditional design for its forms, it is not all that different from some of the rustic furniture that was designed at the turn of the century for the camps of bankers in the Adirondacks, except that it is more whimsical. When bankers like J. P. Morgan went to their mountain camps, they enjoyed rustic furniture, but it was plainer than the "Black Forest" furniture with its delightful animal details.

Marvin D Schwartz

MARVIN D SCHWARTZ

ABOVE:
Birds and other creatures of the wild adorn "Black Forest" furnishings.

OPPOSITE:
A walnut side chair from the last quarter of the nineteenth century, this piece has an open arched back carved with branches, encircling a standing bear.

LEFT:
The nineteenth-century Swiss tendency to incorporate bears and foliage into furniture, as revealed in this side chair, may have had its roots in the medieval tradition of the Wildman, who symbolized the ideals of life as embodied in nature.

ear furniture is frequently described in antique-furniture circles as being the product of the Black Forest in Bavaria, West Germany. This supposition has never been seriously challenged, as forests are the bear's natural habitat, and the thought that this furniture came from the Black Forest is a romantic one that enhances its marketability. Research, including an investigation of the family of original carvers, has established that bear furniture has never been manufactured in Bavaria. It is solely a Swiss product. The misattribution apparently grew from the fact that in the second half of the nineteenth century, Black Forest cabinetmakers manufactured a range of carved cuckoo clocks that were fitted with imported Swiss movements. Later, a similar range of clock cases was produced in Switzerland, which blurred the distinction between the wares of the two regions as components were interchanged. But even though the place of origin of bear furniture is Switzerland rather than the Black Forest, the latter term has long been used by collectors, and it would be confusing to change it now.

Bear furniture originated as a hobby undertaken by a Swiss family of cabinetmakers and wood-carvers named Trauffer, whose members carved at home in the winter evenings to supplement their incomes as teachers at the Brienz carving school. It was therefore a cottage, or rather chalet, industry that developed around the family fire. Mr. F. Peter Trauffer, the first of the family carvers, while selling his finished pieces from door to door, gradually began to reserve some items for the summer tourist trade, which responded enthusiastically to what it perceived as a distinctly regional genre that would certainly astonish and amuse house guests back home. As so often happens with a regional art form, appreciation came initially from outside the community. Although other carvers did contribute to the genre, it remained largely a Trauffer family preserve from the 1880s until the 1950s, when the fourth generation of family members tired of it. Local furniture manufacturers now paid a higher hourly rate, one that made part-time employment less appealing.

The bear's basic form could be hewn from a section of a tree trunk relatively quickly, after which it was left to dry for several months before the detailing was commenced. (Under examination, some larger bear pieces are seen to be comprised of two sections, a fact cleverly disguised in the subsequent staining operation.) The linden tree was preferred for most bear furniture, as it is easy to carve. Walnut was reserved for more ambitious commissions. Almost all pieces were left unsigned, although some were identified with the first initials of the carver's name.

On completion, most bear furniture and sculpture was sold on the spot for cash, often right at the carver's door, which eliminated the need to pack and transport it. Items were often made one at a time and duplicated only after the first one had sold. The vast majority of purchasers were American tourists and servicemen; the latter, according to one of Peter Trauffer's grandchildren, carried off the lion's share of the area's total production after the World Wars (especially World War II). A survey of Swiss and southern German museums and historical societies reveals no examples of bear furniture, which gives credence to the family's contention that it was always primarily a tourist industry.

The brown bear is an emblem of the canton of Bern, Switzerland's capital, appearing not only in the city's official coat of arms but practically everywhere, including building façades, public statuary, and fountains. Indigenous to the forests of the area, the bear was a natural subject for local professional wood-carvers, some of whom taught at the regional carving school (*Schnitzlerschule*), which was founded in Brienz, one hundred kilometers from Bern, in 1884, and others of whom took to the craft as hobbyists. In addition to its presence in the immediate proximity, the bear was also an easy subject to carve, owing to its large and rather amorphous shape, unlike local deer, moose, and farm animals, many of which had long slender legs that required both advanced sculpting craftsmanship and time—impractical commodities for a carver working in his spare time. In addition, students at Brienz were sent on field trips to the bear pit at the Bern zoo, where they were instructed to observe the animals' mannerisms and to sharpen their carving skills. All of this helped to establish

This late-nineteenth-century desk takes its form from traditional eighteenth-century rococo *bureau plats. In this example, the serpentine molded top is incised with meandering branches and raised on cabriole legs carved with a playful cub scampering up a branch.*

the bear as an integral part of the local artistic tradition.

Bears were incorporated into an endless repertoire of centerpieces, chairs, settees, umbrella and plant stands, tables, blanket chests, and armoires. Hugely engaging, but impossible to find nowadays, was an edition of bear chairs that incorporated music boxes beneath the seat. These were activated by a protruding pin, providing observers with vast amusement when an unsuspecting sitter lowered him- or herself into the chair. Another Victorian chair model, virtually unknown today, incorporated a seat under which was housed a child's chamber pot.

While bears were the most identifiable of the subjects carved by three generations of Trauffers, a family catalogue published around 1900 reveals a broad range of freestanding sculpture and miscellaneous household accessories, including wild and domestic animals, birds, garden gnomes, music boxes, nutcrackers, trays, and cuckoo clocks. Many of these are heavily rendered in a romantic baroque style that to modern eyes crosses the line into kitsch.

BELOW AND OPPOSITE:
Although the overall design for this Swiss-made settee is similar to many, this example, with its jovial bear amid chip-carved leafy branches, differs from others in that the arms terminate in bear heads and the legs incorporate bobcatlike masks.

A related curiosity was provided by a range of items in the form of carved elephants, including plant stands, chandeliers, and seat furniture. These were the particular interest of J. Peter Trauffer's son, Jacob, who also created a series of grandfather clocks ornamented in high and full relief with bears foraging among lush foliage. At the same time, a matching edition of clocks was decorated with eagles and owls perched above a pattern of repeating grape clusters that ran the entire vertical length of the clock case. Jacob remained a fervent carver throughout his life. The family recalls the fierce but unsuccessful attempt it made to prize his carving tools from him when in his last years he was placed in an old-age home.

Today we are amused by the disregard for scale on many pieces of bear furniture and by the animals' openmouthed and almost human grimaces. The Trauffer family is still in the carving business, in addition to which it runs a toy shop in Davos, Switzerland. Bears have not, however, been part of their repertoire for some years.

ABOVE:
The freestanding bears in this Swiss window seat have painted mouths and glass-inset eyes. They support a hinged seat incised with edelweiss, which lifts to conceal a musical mechanism.

RIGHT:
This sculptural armchair, carved in Switzerland during the late nineteenth century, takes the form of a freestanding bear supporting a ledge incised to simulate a stump.

A freestanding bear, long thought to have been associated with the German "Black Forest" school of carving, but actually made in Switzerland, provides the focus for this table lamp.

LEFT:
An amusing smoking stand, this piece takes the form of a bear grasping a leafy branch, which holds aloft two tobacco wells surmounted by bear cubs. The stump-form bowl and twisted branch, which forms a ring, were presumably used for supporting canes. A rare feature is the well revealed by the hinged bear's head, undoubtedly used to conceal expensive tobaccos or possibly spirits.

OPPOSITE:
A common form of "Black Forest" furniture, this pine hall seat is carved with an open back in the form of branches, centering a plank seat, which is supported on two well-carved, freestanding adult bears.

116

ABOVE AND RIGHT:
*This "Black Forest" bench is carved with
two well-defined freestanding bears, which
support a rectangular seat. The open back
incorporates five musically talented bears,
each of which plays an instrument.*

In this "Black Forest" settle, two ferocious freestanding bears are juxtaposed against a more jovial back, carved with two precariously seated bears. They, in turn, appear to be hanging from a limb flanked by two industrious bears carrying logs.

LEFT:
This humorous nineteenth-century "Black Forest" hall chair features a hoop back carved with oak branches, in the center of which is a bear standing amid rocks. The legs are in the form of tree trunks, which reveal baby bears.

OPPOSITE:
One of only a few known to exist, this nineteenth-century sculptural armchair may be the ultimate in "Black Forest" furniture.

This Swiss walnut three-piece mantle gar-
niture includes a clock exuberantly carved
to depict a severed stump laden with ferns,
surrounded by two pheasants, and a pair of
tree-form vase holders, carved with foliage
and a pair of hawks and fitted with cut-
glass trumpet-form vases.

ABOVE:
The peripheral carvings on this Continental barometer are to some extent related to the Swiss rustic carvings illustrated elsewhere in this book, the difference being the stylized neoclassical lyre surround formed by the pair of dolphins that flank the instruments. Dolphins and fruit-filled baskets are subjects associated more with Mediterranean countries than with those in Northern Europe.

ABOVE:
This rare rustic easel, circa 1880, is carved to simulate branches, which support a displayed parrot grasping a ring.

TOP:
This rustic walnut serpentine cigar box is carved with a pair of cock pheasants amid rushes. It dates to the second half of the nineteenth century.

ABOVE:
Naturalism was a trademark of the school of carving in Switzerland during the latter part of the nineteenth century. Boxes frequently took the form of tree stumps and logs and were typically adorned with forest foliage and game.

LEFT:
A mother owl perched on a stump nestling her two chicks is the subject for this European mantle clock, carved in the nineteenth century.

ABOVE:
In this Swiss cabinet, the creator has brought the forest indoors. Carved to resemble a stump, the cupboard is surmounted by two smaller stumps and a pair of pheasants.

BELOW AND OPPOSITE, TOP:
*The ultimate in game-inspired furniture,
this large armoire was executed in the
"Black Forest" style during the height of
the exhibition era. The piece was carved to
simulate bark, and its decorative focus rests
on the hounds and rabbits that adorn the
pediment and doors.*

RIGHT:
This comic nineteenth-century Swiss hall stand is carved in the form of a mother bear standing before a tree, which is fitted with a mirror and supports a playful cub.

FAR RIGHT:
This hall rack differs from most "Black Forest" hall racks in that the carver substituted a spaniel for a bear. The well-carved dog straddles a tree, which protects a frightened cat.

Belle Epoque

These rococo-inspired gilt-bronze and marble four-light candelabra feature mermaidlike children frolicking amid rocks, shells, and bulrushes. These were common eighteenth-century Italian motifs, but the superb casting of each figure suggests France as the country of origin.

OPPOSITE:
This French gilt-bronze figural lamp epitomizes the fluidity and grace characteristic of most art nouveau creations. The image of a tightly clad, curvaceous female figure with long flowing hair is a popular theme reflecting the significance of theatrical women like Loïe Fuller, in the works of Toulouse-Lautrec.

Belle Epoque, that kingly and relentlessly curvilinear high style of the later part of the nineteenth century and the opening moments of the twentieth, was all gilded and polished, and glowed in the half-light of gasoliers.

Vivid and delinquent, savory and conceited, energetic and immoderate, rich and dissonant, romantic and materialistic, opulent and bizarre, the Belle Epoque style had a bewitching and often bewildering addiction to embellishment and sumptuous scale. It ran euphorically from Versaillesque pomposity to romantically licentious historicism to debauches of naturalism, without even the most fleeting concern for either authenticity or uniformity of style but with a profound understanding of sensuality. Its textures were lush, its patterns ecstatic, and its detailing rapturous.

It treated wood like pasta and marble like lard. Its design philosophy was eloquently and elegantly superficial, with thoughts no more profound than a blind faith not only in prosperity and the good life but in passementerie and in deep-piled, deep-buttoned, and deep-fringed upholstery.

If this glorious hymn to excess had little philosophical design point of view, it was all so immensely rich and pleasurable that only the hopelessly dull could be insensitive to its brazen charms; indeed, the Belle Epoque style is as voluptuously seductive as the shapely courtesans who played such key roles in forming the period's tastes.

It is a style that triumphs neither in grace and harmony nor in simplicity and logic but that gives in, hell-bent and happy, to every excess that the stimulus of untold wealth can initiate. And it is blissfully oblivious to the democratic rumblings of the Aesthetic and Arts and Crafts movements, which were to have the period's final say in shaping the world of design as we know it.

Yet the Belle Epoque's well-padded opulence—with its feverishly hyperactive detailing, its extreme passion for ornament, and its decorative conceits of aggressively stylish urbanity quite untroubled by any moderating refinements of taste or fine turns of thought—as it shouts of prosperity, is abundantly festive and expensive and gay; and it has a period charm unequaled by anything since.

John Loring

JOHN LORING

The Belle Epoque painted itself with a bold and colorful brush. Today, as one leafs through contemporary fashion reviews to recapture the era and its highlights, one sees interiors that reflected its fierce pulse and optimism. It was, within the home, a time of conspicuous consumption, in which the opulence and daring novelty of one's furnishings established one's place in fashionable society.

The late Victorians, for all their primness and propriety, were not prim and proper consumers. Their world bustled with industry and commerce, which provided a wealth of goods, both newly manufactured at home and imported from abroad. As they indulged themselves with almost sensual passion and abandon, their homes bulged with the loot of an endless buying spree.

Several factors contributed to this accumulative tendency; most importantly, the industrial revolution, which from the mid-nineteenth century had generated a glut of inexpensive mass-produced goods to cater to an indiscriminating bourgeoisie's whims and social aspirations. The growing consumer market spawned a medley of styles, some inspired by the past and some by the Orient and Europe's expanding colonies. In furniture, the handicraft system faced extinction as technology offered bending, stretching, pouring, and molding processes that added new shapes and materials to the standard repertoire of revival-style pieces that had dominated the earlier part of the century.

Fantasy furniture in the Belle Epoque falls into two broad categories: a rampant Victorian eclecticism and an equally exuberant art nouveau style. In the first category, the prevailing pastiche of styles had by the 1890s bred a hybrid mix of neoclassical furniture ornaments, such as cupids, blackamoors, mermaids, and sensual nymphs, which shared the honors with sumptuous Second Empire velvet draperies and upholstery and a range of bizarre foreign creations, such as Chinese bird cages and ferneries. A romantic and witty tone permeated most of this. Above all, home decorating was an intense and enjoyable pursuit. Vacant corners housed potted asphidistras, which added to a general "overspilled" look. Unfortunately, almost all of these furnishings were unsigned, providing today's researcher with problems of attribution.

Within a generation, this cluttered Victorian look yielded to a spartan modernism that ushered in the high-style art deco linearism that followed the Great War. A 1920 article in *The Studio,* which traced the distance in attitude traveled in the two short decades since the turn of the century, stated that "furniture has an architecture of its own, of which the principles have been gradually evolved down the centuries. These laws cannot be disregarded except at the risk of the gravest mistakes, the chief of which is to make a piece of furniture the fantasy of the hour, and not a lasting thing; tempting its owner, a few years later, to banish it to an attic corner as something intolerable."

In the late 1800s nobody flaunted convention more than the Frenchman Rupert Carabin, whose work can be divided broadly into three phases: a seemingly endless cycle of controversy and confrontation during his lifetime; near total oblivion—if not purgatory—from the moment

The blackamoor supports on this Italian baroque side table stand on their own as sculptural works of art. Made during the 1860s in Italy, the table is the product of a rococo revival that swept through the European continent.

This brightly painted and well-carved sun-flower chair may be the work of a Floren-tine craftsman. The blossoms rest on stems, which seem to grow from a deep green tufted velvet upholstered seat, which in turn is raised on supports carved to simulate long blades of grass. A chair of this type would not have been mass produced, but it could have been part of a suite of sunflower seat furniture made for any number of ec-centric patrons.

of his death in 1932 until the sale at the Hotel Drouot in Paris in 1969 of the collection of Henri Montandon, his first client; and since then, a fervent odyssey by today's art nouveau furniture collectors for *anything* by his hand.

In 1882 Carabin's sculpture *à Republic,* depicting a mortician's moldings, was refused by the Paris Salon; eight years later his bookcase for Montandon (purchased recently by the Musée d'Orsay) was similarly barred, this time by the jury of the Salon des Independants, the very group that had broken away from the Salon of the Societé des Artistes Français to free itself from the constraints of artistic expression that it now applied to Carabin, one of its founding members! Carabin found refuge in a private clientele, including Albert Kahn, a banker who was instumental in the development of the Bois de Boulogne, and Coquelin cadet, of the Comèdie Française. An accomplished sculptor by profession, he took every opportunity to incorporate his carved figures into furniture. This drew the wrath of the critics, who felt that by doing so, he violated both disciplines. In 1901 the critic Gerdeil posed the question on everyone's mind: "Why, in wishing to create figural sculpture, does he put it on the foot of a table or the side of a piano? A piano has no relationship to a nude woman and she, in turn, makes a mockery of it."

In 1891, in his book *Degenerescence,* Max Nordeau gave a blistering review of Carabin's exhibit at that year's Salon, writing that "these staircase banisters on which naked and possessed Furies parade tumultuously, these bookcases on which the decapitated heads of assassins form bases and pilasters—even this table which provides the vision of a gigantic opened book borne by gnomes—constitute a style of, and for, the feverish or damned. If the director-general of Dante's Inferno has a reception room, it must surely be similarly furnished. The creations of Mr. Carabin are not furniture, however, but a nightmare."

Carabin's dominant furniture motif was the nude female, which he incorporated into virtually everything, either in the form of caryatids to support chair seats or tabletops or gigantic statuary perched on top of larger pieces, such as armoires. The fact that these nudes, with their serious facial expressions, upswept chignons, and muscular torsos were a little too vulgar in their heavy realism did not help to promote Carabin's cause. Nor did the open sexuality of some of his subjects—often nubile girls and octopuses combined in contorted pairings or female lovers concealed within a coffret on the lid of which a carved caveat advised the inquisitive, "To remain chaste, leave me closed." An ever-present bestiary of cats, owls, and snakes accompanied these maidens, inviting further comment and conjecture on the fantasies that drove Carabin's creativity.

The degree of hostility aroused at the time by Carabin's furniture surprises present-day observers. Whereas his works are certainly unattractive to some, they are not perceived as morally degenerate or sexually provocative, as they were by the prissy Victorian public. They now generate a sense of intrigue and the wish that they could explain their hidden symbolism.

A different type of symbolism was created by Emile Gallé in his furniture ornamentation, one based on the flora and entomology of his native

ABOVE:
A dew-laden shrub provides an appropriate backdrop for this green-painted leaf-cast armchair.

Lorraine. Dragonflies, snails, and creatures of the night hovered and crawled over everything to evoke the rich imagery which the master from Nancy had developed earlier in his glassware. Grotesque insects and all manner of bugs and "creepy-crawlies" were returned to favor in the decorative arts after a three-hundred-year banishment. The scale of Gallé's fantastical imagery made him a frequent transgressor, however. A critic in *Le Figaro* wrote in 1898 of his entry at that year's Salon, "a fluttering dragonfly, immobilized for an instant, has lent its wings to the proportions of a console: witness the Gallé table supported by three dragonfly bodies. The enlargement of the frail insects to the dimensions of a table leg has transformed them into monstrous creatures . . . " Today, it is the very boldness of their size and unabashed ugliness that enchant the collector.

In 1904, the year that he died, Gallé created his pièce de résistance, a spectacular double bed designed around the theme of Dawn and Dusk (*Aube et Crépuscule*), in which the headboard was veneered with a moth, to symbolize dawn, and the footboard with a fantastic pair of facing dragonflies, representing death, all rendered in glass, mother-of-pearl, and exotic fruitwood marquetry. The position of the bed's two ends—encompassing the mattress on which man is conceived, born, and dies—provided Gallé with perhaps his most powerfully symbolic theme.

In the French capital, furniture in the modern style embraced a more restrained and subtle form of ornamentation, one that clearly took its inspiration from the Belgian architect, Victor Horta. Hector Guimard, in particular, adopted the attenuated and sinuous line introduced in Brussels some years earlier. As a Paris critic noted, "Here is the Horta line in mad exuberance . . . it whips across ground, walls, and ceiling, breaks out of capitals, runs down flights of stairs, spreads through the branches of the chandeliers, creeps across the window leading. It lashes around everywhere, wraps around, intertwines, unties itself, as flexible as a liana—a liana tamed by geometry . . . "

Guimard took the Horta line and made it split the air like a coachman's whip. In so doing, he shook the Parisian architectural establishment to its foundations. It was not so much that he had introduced a highly controversial style—the need for something new, even iconoclastic, preoccupied architects in the 1890s as it did cabinetmakers—but that he flaunted his self-confidence at his antagonists, of whom there were soon many. His buildings, such as the Castel Béranger and the Humbert de Romans music hall, and his entrances for the Métro stations, with their languid *entrelac* curves that turn back on themselves, scandalized Paris. His furniture matched the buildings that housed them. As such, they still generate astonishment. Unlike Gallé and the Ecole de Nancy, Guimard based his designs on a plant's stem rather than on its flower. The resulting long sinuous lines, intersected at intervals by knopped protrusions—presumably the stylized joints from which offshoots emerge—appear as gnarled and natural organisms.

In Spain, Antonio Gaudí interpreted the whiplash art nouveau line to the north of him with a cavalier Mediterranean zest. His prie-dieux for the chapel of the Colonia Güell, for example, executed in 1898,

RIGHT:
Gallé's Vitrine aux Libellules *(see p. 156) and this sumptuous bed, known as the* Aube et Crépuscule, *were both commissioned by Henry Hirsch in 1904. Considered to be Gallé's finest, they are also the last pieces to have been designed by him. Unlike the vitrine, which attests to Gallé's sculptural talents, the* Aube et Crépuscule, *now in the Musée de l'Ecole de Nancy, testifies to his skill and creativity in the use of marquetry. The head and footboard are delicately inlaid with mother-of-pearl and various fruitwoods to form a stylized moth. The translucent wings surround an opal delicately carved with similar dragonflies.*

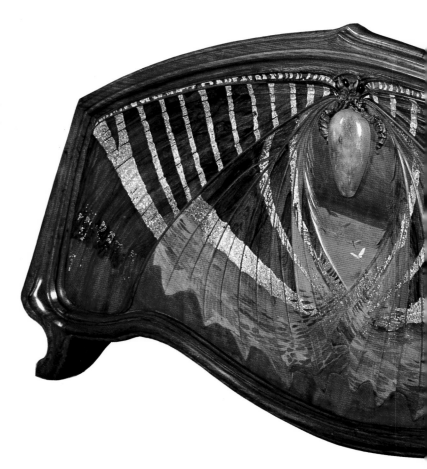

The Renaissance-inspired putto on this nineteenth-century walnut stool sits precariously atop one of the faux bamboo turned supports. He grasps a cloth set between the support to form the seat. The natural folds and fringe on the cloth, the frayed rope that binds the supports, and the realistic splinters and knots set in the "bamboo" all attest to the craftsman's talent as a sculptor as well as a cabinetmaker.

combined visionary design with rigorous cabinetry. In 1906 his furnishings for the Casa Batlló included chairs comprised of double and multiple units that echoed his most eccentric architectural creations.

Throughout his career, Gaudí continued to mix revolutionary art nouveau designs with tradition. The Church of the Sagrada Familia was furnished with stiffly traditional pews and a wooden pulpit, for example, yet the seats in the Parque Güell and Santa Coloma de Cervelló followed a broad, serpentine, art nouveau sweep.

Also in Barcelona, the designer Alejo Clapes Puig turned his hand on occasion to furniture. Clearly influenced by what he had seen while working with Gaudí on the Palau Güell, Clapes appears to have tried to go beyond his mentor. The suite of salon furniture he designed for the Ibarz house in Barcelona (now in the Museo Gaudí) included a vitrine, chairs and portmanteau that are as outrageously art nouveau as one can imagine, with carved drapes and sweeping organic legs that exceeded anything that Paris or Nancy had dared to conceive.

Italian Belle Epoque furniture was dominated by one man, Carlo Bugatti. Except for him, the *style nouille*, as the French were quick to label the vermicelli-like volutes found on Italian architecture at the time, was practically nonexistent. Nobody tried to match his idiosyncratic flair, although Carlo Zen and Eugenio Quarti generated a range of diluted art nouveau furnishings inspired directly by the Paris salons.

Described by the critic Maxime LeRoy in 1903 as "an isolated genius whose flair for the bizarre defies classification," Bugatti carried the art nouveau banner in Italy virtually single-handedly. His interpretation of the new art was utterly unique, drawing on a marvelous hodgepodge of Hispano-Moresque architectural influences painted with Japanese bamboo shoots and other exoticism. Pseudo-Arabic minarets, dentils, and spindled galleries silhouetted the outlines of furniture designed around the circle and its parts—the arc and chord. Wooden frames were covered in chamois leather within repoussé metal mounts or veneered in pewter and brass with insectlike motifs and Middle Eastern calligraphy. Tassels, either singly or in fringes, added to the theatrical effect.

The critics were variously perplexed, excited, or angered. Bugatti reminded his detractors that the price of individualism is that it *is* different. Yet his style was to many ponderous, devoid of the airiness and fluidity that the new style was meant to espouse. One critic, on viewing the bedroom that Lord Battersea had commissioned for his London home around 1900, found that the visit's only merit was that it saved him the cost of a train ride to Granada to see the Alhambra! Bugatti's Snail Room, shown at the Turin Exposition two years later, was better received in its striking modernity. The unbroken sweep of the chairs resembled an upended snail. The walls of the room picked up on the theme, with repeating bands of large circular panels that resembled the mollusk's back, beneath which ran a long undulating couch.

LEFT AND BELOW:
A bundle of loose cloth grasped by floating putti forms the design for this eighteenth-century-inspired, highly entertaining walnut and fruitwood Venetian child's cradle. The polished surface adds to the overall delight evoked by a subject appropriately selected for this aristocratic whimsy.

By the outbreak of World War I, the Belle Epoque's glitter had long since faded. With it, the furniture of the era passed into memory, and to many, this happened not a moment too soon. Certainly nothing as shamelessly exuberant or unselfconscious was attempted for another eighty years, until the vibrant Memphis style was launched in Milan. Today, we have forgiven the turn of the century its excesses to the point, even, that we welcome them as lively, even necessary, accents for modern interiors.

RIGHT:
Aquatic subjects were popular motifs for jardinieres. This majolica pair, probably made by the French porcelain designer A. Deck in the 1880s, is formed as a krater molded with a pair of dolphin-headed sea serpents. Each pedestal is adorned with three bearded creatures, which spring from a water-laden rockwork base. The artist chose to striate the turquoise glaze, thus heightening the overall nautical effect.

RIGHT:
Attributable to the English firm of Minton and Co., this handsome jardiniere, on a matching stand, is brightly painted with a peacock on a deep blue ground. Majolica jardinieres like this one were a great success and took numerous prizes at the Crystal Palace Exhibition of 1851.

LEFT:
This late-nineteenth-century Italian porcelain whatnot takes the form of an oversized bunch of ribbon-tied daisies, modeled and pruned to form a monumental reticulated ewer.

OPPOSITE:
The finest Italian Carrara marble was used for this exquisite console table. The sculptor, working in a classical tradition, chose a pair of attenuated whippets, headed by Ionic capitals and seated before drapery swags, to support a rectangular frieze carved with a traditional neoclassical plaque flanked by foliage.

RIGHT:
In this Venetian armchair, en suite with the double-chair-back settee, the padded back is surmounted by a single blackamoor child seated before a peaked cloth painted with foliage and scrolls; the downswept arms are raised on blackamoor supports, in the center of which is an upholstered seat. The painted cabriole legs carved with pendant drapes are a simplification of the blackamoor supports on the settee.

ABOVE AND OPPOSITE, TOP LEFT:
*Moorish influence on the European conti-
nent manifested itself in architecture, and it
also played an important role in the decorative schemes of Venetian furniture. The
numerous blackamoors and the
polychrome-painted draperies carved on
this amusing nineteenth-century double-
chair-back Venetian settee resemble those
on settees produced during the seventeenth
and eighteenth centuries.*

LEFT:
The European search for an exotic folly was realized in this pair of impressive brass palm trees. They date to the early part of the nineteenth century and would potentially fit into Henry Holland's overall decorative scheme for the Prince of Wales's Pavilion at Brighton. Each shaped palm frond is individually set in a segmented trunk and appears to float as freely as a natural palm. In this photograph, the trees flank a Napoleon III gilt-decorated papier-mâché armchair made in France between 1855 and 1870.

LEFT:
The marble-inset giltwood side table illustrated here incorporates motifs used in England, France, and Italy. The shell-carved frieze and leaf-laden supports are drawn from early-eighteenth-century prototypes. Used in a foyer, it may have had a mirror carved en suite and a pair of flanking baroque sculptural torchères.

OPPOSITE:
Bordellos were legalized in France in 1802, but not until 1878 was one of high standing, Chabanais, opened several paces from the Bibliothèque Nationale at 12 rue Chabanais. This establishment, founded by the refined and gracious Madame Kelly, soon grew to be the most celebrated in the world and was thought by foreign visitors to be one form of the rayonnant français. The Chief of Protocol of L'Élysée was even known to arrange visits to this most famous of the maisons de tolerance for foreign sovereigns. According to sources in Paris, one such dignitary, the future king of England, Edward VII, did not simply make a one-time appearance but had his own furniture created for his use. This siège d'amour, made to measure by M. Soubrier in 1890, was complete with stirrups and designed to allow Edward to amuse himself with two ladies at the same time. Made in the rococo style, the gilded and painted wood love chair sold for 32,000 francs in a 1951 sale by Maître Rheims.

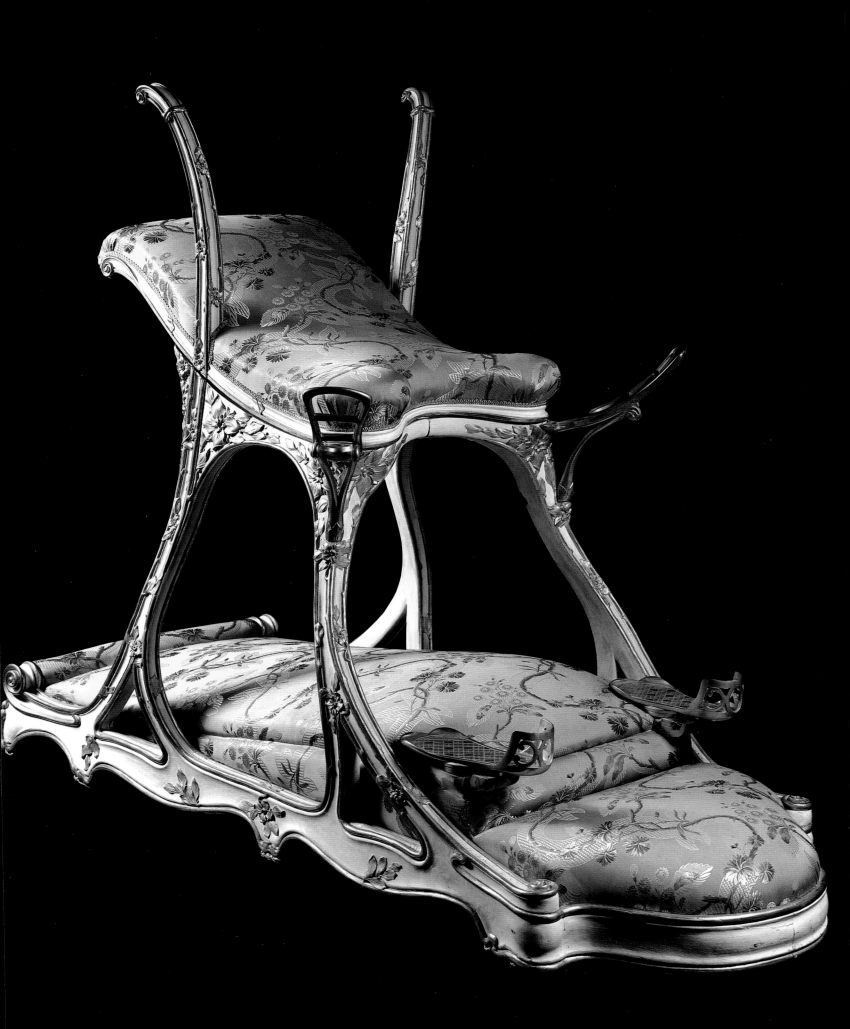

ABOVE:
This most unusual bronze humidor epitomizes the 1880s taste for exoticism. It takes the form of four elephants standing back to back in a circle before recessed oval basins interspersed with scrolls; the elephants support a covered cylindrical cup with two projecting arms surmounted by bobeche. Although its country of origin is anyone's guess, the superior quality of its casting and imaginative form warrants comparison to the 1880s works of art cast by the French firm of Barbedienne.

ABOVE:
This late-nineteenth-century gilt-bronze-mounted earthenware centerpiece incorporates a bowl manufactured by the Hungarian firm of Zsolnay. Made from a material commonly called Ivoir-Fayence, *this particular piece is decorated with gilt and painted foliage in imitation of earlier Persian Isnick pottery.*

OPPOSITE:
This architecturally inspired parcel-gilt mahogany bird cage may have been designed for a late-nineteenth-century exhibition. It is surmounted by many rounded roofs, incorporates arches, and is fitted with a Gothic rose window.

ABOVE:
The three giltwood swans wading though aquatic foliage on the base of this nineteenth-century plant stand provide a picture-perfect foil for the cascade of green leaves that would have dangled from its reticulated oval basket.

PRECEDING PAGES:
Not all late-nineteenth-century French interiors were as lavishly decorated as this heavily draped, eccentric parlor in Paris, furnished with "tube" upholstered chairs and settees, which were reupholstered by Yves Marthelot.

LEFT:

A French brothel, a lady's boudoir, or an opera set for La Traviata *would all serve as appropriate settings for this richly upholstered tête-à-tête, designed by the contemporary Parisian designer Yves Marthelot.*

ABOVE:

Upholstery played an extremely important role in the overall decorative schemes of the nineteenth century. This unusual jardiniere, on a matching stand, made in the twentieth century by Yves Marthelot in Paris, is upholstered in multicolored coiled velvet.

LEFT:

Although this settee takes the form of a nineteenth-century rococo revival love seat, it has been completely reupholstered with multicolored coiled velvet by Yves Marthelot of Paris.

ABOVE:
A Venetian wall appliqué with a mirror-framed oval surround encloses a painted earthenware harlequin. The comic figure grasps a hand-blown glass two-light torch decorated with stylized flowers and wreaths. It is one of a pair made during the latter part of the nineteenth century.

RIGHT:
Although tall case clocks had been in existence for two hundred years prior to the creation of this French art nouveau example, few seem to possess the sensuality and dreamlike qualities manifested in the overall fluid contours of the case, carved with a woodland nymph amid evergreens. The cresting is surmounted by a rooster, a fitting allegory for this time piece. The inscription reads Toutes s'envont on ne peut prolonger la meilleuze.

OPPOSITE:
This Turkish-inspired dry sink was made by the Italian designer Carlo Bugatti, who worked between 1890 and 1920. His chairs and cabinets were usually based on architectural or organic forms and painted in high-gloss finishes which incorporated delicate pewter or ivory inlays with metal or parchment mounts. In this example, a spindle-inset gallery is fitted with small drawers; the rectangular surface opens to a fitted well and is inlaid with pewter to form Islamic script. The arched façade is mounted with reticulated copper plaques.

LEFT:
Exhibited by Carabin in 1893 at the Société Nationale des Beaux-Arts, this sensational chair surely caused a stir. Made from walnut, Carabin's preferred material, it incorporates a buxom kneeling woman affixed to the chair back. The plank seat supports a cat, seemingly enthralled with its master.

OPPOSITE:
Signed R. Carabin *and dated 1896, this walnut chair incorporates his two favorite images, cats and a female nude. Hanging from a sash, the buxom, broad-hipped woman appears to melt into the chair back, which surrounds two curious cats.*

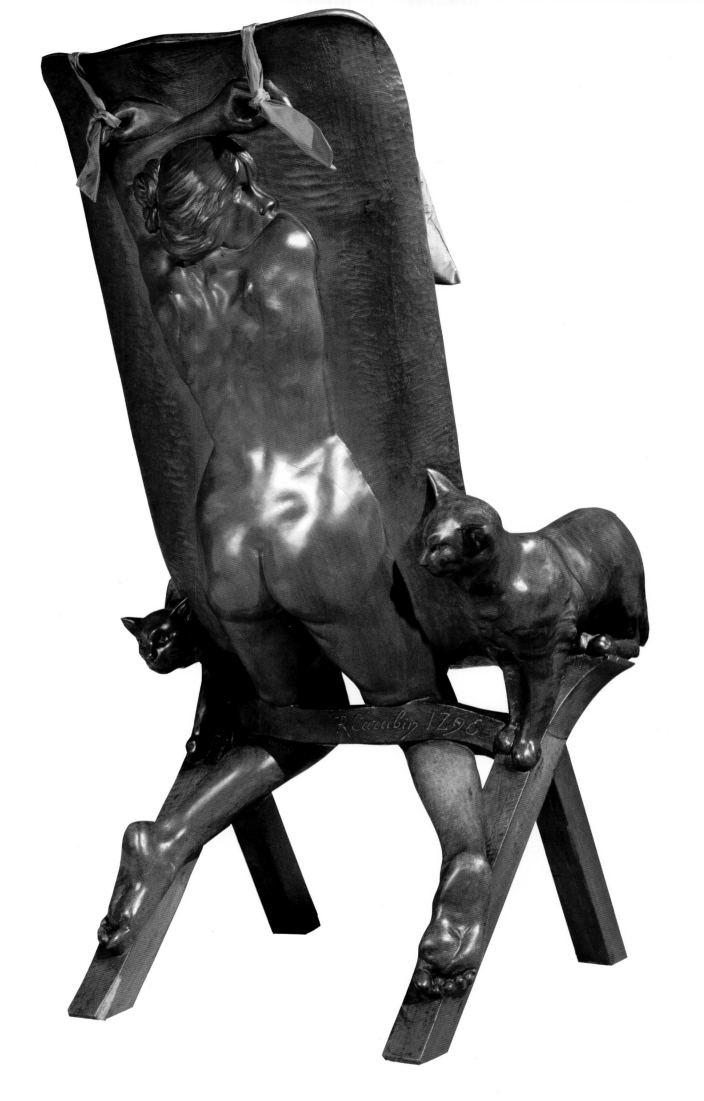

155

LEFT:
Made in 1904 and considered to be one of Emil Gallé's greatest creations, this awesome work of art is known as the Vitrine aux Libellules. *The somber molded glazed rectangular superstructure sits majestically upon an ironwood and oak base carved with surreal dragonflies with iridescent glass-inset eyes.*

OPPOSITE:
Rupert Carabin appears to have been a sculptor as well as a great ébéniste. *He was the creator of this enchanting* bibliothèque, *now in the Musée D'Orsay, signed* Carabin *and dated 1890. Made from walnut with iron cattails and palm fronds, the rectangular case incorporates figures in relief as well as in the round. The females poised atop the case may be allegorical figures or merely woodland nymphs.*

This French walnut floriform plant stand was made during the height of the art nouveau movement. It is an example of how the proponents of art nouveau reacted against the academic historicism of the second half of the nineteenth century. It takes the form of lily pads which support a central bud, now fitted to hold a candle. Although it is sculptural, it bears similarities to the delicate floral marquetry and the overlaid flowers cut into glass designed by Emil Gallé.

OPPOSITE:
Nature provided the inspiration for this French art nouveau armchair in the style of Louis Majorelle, with its central panel of carved foliage. The plasticity of the chair's surround and supports are also characteristics typical of the art nouveau style.

LEFT:
A bold defiance of symmetry and a comical plantlike quality best characterize this Gaudiesque mahogany armchair. In this chair, the circular molded back with chip-carved foliage centers similarly carved ear-like sides. The conforming plank seat is raised on an interlaced rootlike tripod support terminating in stylized hooved feet. This surreal-looking chair is an example of Spanish art nouveau.

ABOVE:

The French sculptor, architect, and designer Hector Guimard may be responsible for this surreal mahogany and maple lounge chair. It was created around the turn of the century, about the same time as his greatest achievement, the Paris Métro stations. It is a tour de force of slithery plasticlike asymmetrical lines typically associated with the style sometimes called "le style Guimard" or "le style bouche de Métro" but universally known as art nouveau.

RIGHT:

This ormolu table was cast in adherence to the aesthetic guidelines fashionable in the 1890s. The onyx top rests on a circular tapering stand cast with stylized leaves characteristic of the plasticity of art nouveau metalwork. Although its uses are limitless, it may have originally been wrought for one of Paris's many cafés.

Materials

It has been my great pleasure as chairman and principal auctioneer for Sotheby's to have studied and sold some of the world's finest examples of furniture. Through their materials—the surprising details, exotic fragments, and bold designs—these pieces have taught us a great deal about the social history and creative instincts of man. They serve as visual records of their centuries and as a continuing chronicle of our time.

Beginning in the sixteenth century, furniture style was profoundly influenced by the craftsman's materials as he began to experiment with the notion of adornment. The use of simple yet extraneous materials, such as ivory and colored stone, is evident in some of the earlier examples of ornamentation; for example, the elegant use of pietra dura in Italy. By the seventeenth century, however, the art of adornment became firmly established as furniture style was dominated by the lavish tastes of the French court at Versailles. The expressions of royal ceremony and splendor are reflected in the richly embellished commodes by Boulle encrusted with luxurious metals and tortoiseshell inlays. As the eighteenth century progressed, furniture design and ornamentation continued to accept inspiration from court life, adding the exquisite detailing of marquetry and parquetry in wood and elaborate inlays using mother-of-pearl and lacquer. Finally, by the nineteenth century, imagination and invention took hold as more unusual materials once reserved only for decoration became the very substance of construction. Furniture design around the world was now dominated by the creative use of materials in pieces fabricated entirely of exotic materials such as horn and antler, found in Scandinavia, Northern Europe, England, and America, and papier-mâché, found in France and England.

Throughout the history of furniture making, the spirit of the times has been reflected in the distinctive style and preferred materials of each period. I am sure you will be as fascinated as I have been about what follows in this chapter.

John Marion

JOHN L. MARION

OPPOSITE AND RIGHT:
A whimsical patinated bronze and copper crane poses amid meandering vines. This standing floor lamp dates to the turn of the twentieth century and could have been made anywhere on the European continent.

الصدق عماد الدين

The shade of this "jewel"-encrusted reticu-lated patinated copper floor lamp warrants a comparison to two short-lived, late-nineteenth-century artistic fads. Its overall form, is somewhat reminiscent of a Moor-ish mosque lamp, while the stylized floral motifs that adorn the shade and standard relate to the foliage characteristic of art nouveau naturalism.

ABOVE:
Small decorative teakwood whimsies like this figural stand were used in England to decorate rooms with exotic themes. The wooden camel supports a foliate-carved oc-tagonal top and may have stood alongside a Middle Eastern settee in a room with an overall Islamic theme.

LEFT:
The European craze to create Islamic smoking dens during the latter part of the nineteenth century led to the manufactur-ing in the Middle East of decorative fur-nishings like this triple chair-back settee. A myriad of bone, ivory, ebony, and mother-of-pearl inlays and beads form the overall geometric pattern common to all Islamic-inspired furniture.

LEFT:
This highly stylized early-nineteenth-century gilt-decorated black lacquer recamier draws its inspiration in part from earlier Italian baroque whimsies and from Chinese export lacquer. With shell decor and dragons' feet, this recamier would have been suitable for the Prince of Wales's Brighton Pavilion, where a similar one graces the salon.

OPPOSITE:
This most unusual foliage-carved arm-chair is signed Trougniou Ancien Facteur *and dated 1858. The material used is teakwood; one could therefore presume its origin to be Southeast Asia. The chair bears the arms of Napoleon III and is further decorated with a military trophy. It may have been a gift to the French monarch or to someone within his inner circle.*

RIGHT:
This Scandinavian cork-veneered arm-chair is a product of the rustic movement that swept through the United States and Europe during the late nineteenth and early twentieth centuries.

ABOVE:
This mid-nineteenth-century antler-mounted standish is from Bavaria.

LEFT:
The late nineteenth century saw a revival of pewter as a fashionable metal for domestic wares. This ovoid pitcher is cast in the form of a rooster's head and is a product of the Arts and Crafts movement, which spread through Europe in reaction to the opulence typically associated with the decorative arts of the late nineteenth century.

RIGHT:
Urns were used to line walkways in large, carefully executed European gardens. In this polished steel example, one of a pair, the krater-shaped bowl is cast with two pairs of entwined serpents, which form the handles.

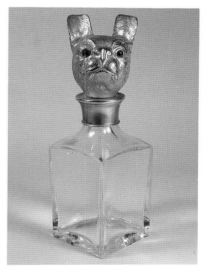

ABOVE AND TOP LEFT:
The inkwell and decanter both date to the early part of this century. The former is fitted with a hinged brass lid cast in the form of an elephant's head, with glass-inset eyes and ivory tusks; the latter is fitted with a brass stopper cast to simulate a stylized pug dog. Both are English and presumably part of a large set.

LEFT:
Although this mother-of-pearl- and ebony-inlaid chair is a modern copy, many of this type were made in India during the twentieth century as adaptations of English Regency chairs. All incorporated rams' heads and have saber legs, but some are mounted with silver and brass, while others are veneered in ivory.

Wicker

Often misunderstood, *wicker* is the generic term correctly used to describe *all* woven items, including those made of rattan, cane, reed, willow, palm, raffia, fiber (spun wood pulp), rush, and various dried grasses. As such, its usefulness and appeal are infinite: Not only is it light, pliable, and inexpensive, but when fashioned with Victorian ingenuity, it became practical and highly ornate.

Within the wicker family, rattan has proved itself the most versatile material for furniture production. A climbing palm or vine indigenous to the East Indies—in particular, Borneo and the Malaysian archipelago—rattan winds its way up neighboring trees to attain a height of five hundred feet or more, without exceeding 1 1/2 inches in diameter. On being cut and trimmed, it provides wicker manufacturers with three primary elements of their trade: the rattan pole itself for furniture supports, such as chair feet and backrests; cane (the long thin strips of the outer bark), used to weave chair seats and backs; and reed (the inner bark or pith), used because of its special pliancy for intricately matted and rope-twist ornamentation. These, in combination with other wicker materials, provide manufacturers with unlimited ornamental effects.

Perhaps surprisingly, it was in the United States that wicker was developed fully as a decorative furniture form. In England and Europe, where it was first imported during the China Trade, it had been perceived as a functional material, for which, as in the Orient of antiquity, it was used to produce rather lackluster household furnishings. Fortunately, by 1860, when America's production of wicker had exceeded that of Europe, its potential in its land of adoption was enthusiastically recognized, and it was used widely in gardens and porches, in the form of settees, rockers, and plant stands. From there it was a short step to the bird cages, music stands, phonograph cabinets, bassinets, and host of knickknacks and exotica that flooded late-nineteenth-century American drawing rooms and bedrooms. The country became unashamedly wild about wicker as the medium's potential catered fully to the Victorian taste for eclecticism.

By the late 1880s, when wicker was at its most popular, a host of revival and exotic styles vied for the homeowner's attention and pocketbook: in particular, rococo, Elizabethan, Moorish, Gothic, Chinese, and Italian Renaissance. Wicker's unique characteristics of airiness and whimsy provided these varied styles with a fresh look enhanced by the material's ability to be coaxed into any imaginable shape. C-scrolls, curlicues, and arabesques created a particularly novel decorative appeal. Gilding, painting, and shellacking allowed a wider range of effects, as did the application of colorful cotton bows and sashes.

OPPOSITE:
Produced in the late nineteenth and early twentieth centuries, wicker furniture adorned many porches, conservatories, and summer retreats. This French example is woven in an overall complex pattern of interlaced braids.

RIGHT:
Affixed to a bamboo tripod stand, this two-toned wicker basket, woven in the form of a cornucopia, could have been the product of a number of firms in France, England, or America. It dates to the latter part of the nineteenth century and originally served as a plant stand.

The wicker industry in the United States dates to 1844, when a young Bostonian, Cyrus Wakefield, observed a bundle of rattan being thrown overboard from a clipper ship. The rattan served as dunnage to prevent the cargo from shifting on its long voyage from the Orient. Retrieving the bundle, Wakefield experimented with the material to determine its possibilities for chair production. From this modest beginning was spawned the giant Wakefield Rattan Company, established in East Reading (later named Wakefield in honor of the factory and its founder), Massachusetts, in 1855, where Wakefield's first wicker pieces were manufactured. The next fifty years witnessed the growth and maturity of the wicker industry in the United States, culminating in the merger in 1897 of its two giants, the Wakefield Rattan Company and Heywood Bros. & Company, of Boston, to form the Heywood Wakefield Company. During this time other firms, including department stores such as Sears Roebuck and Montgomery Ward, helped to cater to the broad domestic demand.

Wicker remained in vogue from the Civil War until the late 1920s, when its popularity abruptly waned. Its downfall was partly due to the invention of the Lloyd loom, which produced a closely woven but basic wicker matted pattern that, while multiplying output, made consumers aware that the medium's earlier handcraftsmanship was now absent. In addition, from the early 1900s Gustav Stickley and other Arts and Crafts cabinetmakers offered wicker furniture in a restrained Mission style, in stark contrast to the overtly embellished decoration with which it had been associated but which now seemed increasingly vulgar and outmoded as a new angular modernism came into vogue.

ABOVE:
Suitable for a picnic but probably used for storing sewing implements, this charming wicker ladies' work basket dates from the 1830s to 1850s and may have been made in England.

ABOVE AND BELOW:
*These nineteenth-century oriental fu dogs
are carved from a single root.*

Root & Twig

Rustic furniture, comprised of a tree's components—the branches, trunk, roots, and twigs—first appeared in Europe in the mid-eighteenth century in chair designs for arbors and gazebos in landscaped gardens. Its composition of roots and branches gave it the appearance of a living organism that blended perfectly into its environment.

Rustic furniture reached to the core of the Victorian's ambivalence concerning his industrial success. As the essayist Robert van Court aptly summarized in his 1912 *Vacation Homes in the Woods*, " . . . to those of us who live and work amid the artificiality of city life, there is something irresistibly attractive in the idea of being close to the heart of nature, wearing old clothes and living for a time the free and easy life which we like to imagine was lived before the call of the city became insistent." Mother Nature—which urban man had foresaken in the stampede to modernization—was perceived now with nostalgia, the source of an ardent pantheism that alone could salvage him from the city's moral and spiritual turpitude.

By the early 1800s the virtues of rusticity were continually extolled by city dwellers, who used root and twig furniture to furnish their arcadian retreats, including country houses and more modest weekend cottages and log cabins. This appreciation was absent in the rural communities themselves, where poverty precluded the choice of more fashionable (and comfortable) surroundings.

Nineteenth-century rustic furniture varied widely in interpretation, ranging from a restrained, almost neoclassical look in which twigginess was combined with neatness, to a more robust naturalism in which untamed roots, twigs, and branches sprouted willy-nilly on chair backs and table legs. Unlike most furniture, in which cabinetmakers disguise the natural features of the wood, makers of rustic furniture went to the extreme of promoting the material's imperfections. Burls and knots were highlighted to promote a gnarled and unhewn naturalism. Often the shape of the branches and roots dictated the basic form of the piece, in direct violation of the canons of traditional cabinetry. Violators reminded their critics that nature abhorred a straight line.

Ideas for Rustic Furniture, published in the late eighteenth century in London for I. & J. Taylor's architectural library, contained twenty-six plates that showed twig furniture carefully trimmed to ensure symmetry. The book inspired the German review, *Ideenmagazin,* which reproduced several plates for an article that helped to revive enthusiasm for the related genre of antler furniture. In the United States, the rustic style became a regional handicraft, primarily in the Blue Mountain Lake area of the Adi-

Bernard Palissy's rustic earthenwares, produced in France during the middle of the sixteenth century, provided the inspiration for this highly unusual Royal Doulton earthenware chair. The chair takes the form of a severed tree, with broken branches rising from a stump. The surface is worked to simulate bark, and the overall effect of a dying tree is heightened by the addition of painted beetles, fungi, shells, leaves, and snakes. This oddity is the epitomy of nineteenth-century naturalism.

RIGHT:
Chairs like this nineteenth-century root and bamboo example were the rage among the English gentry striving to produce a rustic effect on the premises of their country homes. In this mid-nineteenth-century armchair, lacquered gnarled roots are affixed to pieces of bamboo which form star motifs within diagonal borders.

LEFT:
As the demand for garden furniture and rustic ornaments grew, amateurs tried their luck at creating picturesque whimsies used to furnish their own country lodges. This simple nineteenth-century pedestal with its gnarled root support is one of these whimsies created by a hobbyist.

RIGHT:
Victorian England's passionate wooing of nature prompted the manufacture of numerous rustic curiosities. This bamboo-mounted fernery with its Japanese-inspired root support is but one example of the picturesque in a larger framework of romanticism.

rondacks and in Appalachian summer camps, which enjoyed a brisk popularity among vacationers well into this century. In the Adirondacks, a rather untwiglike style of rustic furniture evolved, one in which veneers of white and yellow birch bark were juxtaposed to provide distinctive surface patterns.

Rustic furniture remains an endearing, and often witty, style that intrigues today's viewer more by its inventive quirkiness than by its ability to entice an urbanite back to his or her primordial roots.

ABOVE:
Swiss, German, Austrian, or English, this rustic-inspired walnut hall rack was created during the second half of the nineteenth century. The triangular upper section features a mirror within a surround carved with branches and hanging grapevines. The standard incorporates cattails and is affixed to a pair of branch-carved supports.

ABOVE:
This simple bamboo-woven rustic center table incorporates a Japanese-inspired root base, which supports an elongated top decorated with split bamboo arranged in a pattern of diamonds and scrolls.

ABOVE:
This Japanese-inspired fire screen has a central panel, embroidered with an eagle perched on a pine tree, set against a distant landscape, all within a gnarled root surround.

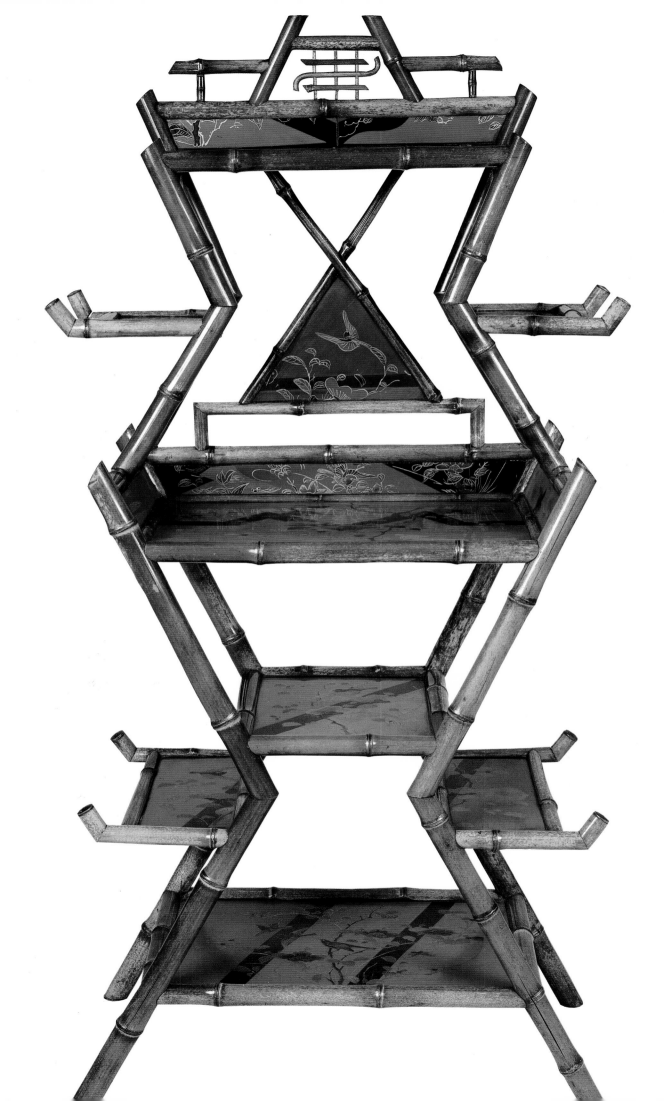

The West's captivation with the Orient reached its height in the 1750s and 1760s, spurred in part by two 1754 publications, Chippendale's *Gentleman and Cabinetmaker's Director* and Edwards & Darly's *New Book of Chinese Designs,* both of which illustrated a cross section of Chinese furnishings ranging in style from a formal banality to great exuberance. Three years later, Sir William Chambers's 1757 volume, *Chinese Designs of Buildings, Furniture, Dresses, Machines and Utensils* further whetted the Europeans' insatiable thirst for Orientalia. Although Chambers asserted that his illustrations could be used as prototypes for English cabinetmakers, the low cost of furniture production in China appears to have dissuaded the local industry from producing either real or *faux* bamboo items.

By the 1790s this cult had faded, but it was revived abruptly by the Prince Regent's creation of the Brighton Pavilion. Included within this fantastic structure was a Chinese gallery, inspired by the gift to the Prince of a set of Chinese wallpapers. Another room with painted glass walls was contrived as a Chinese lantern. Although the Prince Regent had previously incorporated a Chinese room in Carlton House, Buckinghamshire, this new interpretation of chinoiserie, created with brilliant colors and exuberant decoration, surpassed in splendor anything that preceded it.

In the early 1800s imported Chinese bamboo furniture was elaborately conceived, with compact caned latticework construction and lacquered surfaces, unlike that for the domestic Chinese market, which was stout and rudimentary. For the European market, protruding joints and feet were neatly capped in ivory, bone, or metal.

Bamboo's versatility was readily appreciated in England. It was exceedingly light, but despite this seeming fragility, it could be readily strengthened by combining single elements. Chair legs, for example, were composed of several lengths of bamboo rods pinned or bound together, rather than a single growth. The largest importer was the East India Company, which sold its cargo by auction at its headquarters in Leadinghall, St. Mary's, London. In competition were a large number of independent importers who sold to shops from their wholesale warehouses.

Several English cabinetmakers responded to the continuing public demand by producing both real and simulated (*faux*) bamboo furnishings. The London firm of Edward, Marsh, & Tatham generated a large volume of both real and simulated bamboo, often mixing imported lacquered panels and rattan fretwork with beech rods turned and tinted in imitation of bamboo shoots. Gillows and Howard & Sons of Berner Street, Lon-

ABOVE:
Bamboo furniture became popular in England during the middle of the eighteenth century with the publication in 1757 of William Chamber's Designs for Chinese Buildings, Furniture, Etc. *This nineteenth-century armchair incorporates a Japanese lacquer panel within a surround of woven rattan. The shaped bamboo cresting and lattice-filled arms are architectural elements prevalent in many Chinese pavilions.*

OPPOSITE:
As the English and French imported large quantities of bamboo from the Orient, nineteenth-century furniture makers were assured a readily available source for household goods. Inexpensive yet fashionable, this etagere, possibly made by the English firm W.T. Ellmore & Son *in the 1880s, incorporates Japanese lacquer panels set into a bamboo frame.*

don, offered a similar selection of "occasional" pieces—washstands, side chairs, and bedroom furniture—inspired in part by a set of tables and a supper canterbury, designed by Sheraton in the 1770s and 1780s, with out-turned feet turned to simulate bamboo moldings. In the United States, where bamboo had been imported since the China Trade accord of 1784, a Boston cabinetmaker, Samuel Gragg, in 1809 advertised fancy and common chairs and settees made of maple. Toward the end of the century, George Huntzinger, a German immigrant located in New York City, produced a range of formal *faux* bamboo furniture with turned and spindled frames supporting upholstered and cushioned seats.

The 1860s heralded the mania for *japonisme* that swept England in the second half of the Victorian era and that, in turn, helped to usher in the Aesthetic movement. Waves of imported lacquered wares, bronzes, and prints prompted English manufacturers to capitalize on the style's popularity, adopting it throughout the applied arts. The distinction between Chinese and Japanese decoration was quickly blurred. Bamboo furniture was suddenly "Japanese," despite the fact that European-style conventional furniture was superfluous (beyond a range of small screens and household accessories) in a country where "people sat upon their heels or lay upon the floor." Homeowners, however, appeared totally unconcerned with such contradictions, delighting in the fanciful range of "Japanese" seat furniture produced between 1869 and 1935 by roughly 150 registered English bamboo manufacturers. In London, these included, most notably, Hubert Bill of Little Camden Street, Daniel Jacobs & Sons of Hackney Road, C.C. Beetles of New North Road, and P. Bastendorff & Company of Euston Square.

Manufacturers adorned such Victorian bamboo curiosities as "cosy corners," musical tea tables, fern stands, and whatnots with an imaginative mix of ornamentation. Enthusiasm for novelty often spilled over into combination pieces, such as desk-cabinet-jardiniere-lamps, from which even the average acquisitive Victorian homeowner shied away. Beyond London, bamboo was made in Birmingham, where W. F. Needham excelled, and in Leicester and Nottingham. Very few of these makers bothered to stamp or label their products, providing difficulties for today's collectors, as methods of bamboo construction have been universally standard since the Sung dynasty (966–1279).

Bamboo was also exported to the United States from France. French bamboo differed from the English variety. It was frequently stained in a wide range of colors, and was generally heavier in appearance, with richer decoration and textile upholstery. The best known and most prolific manufacturer of bamboo furnishings in France was the firm of Perret & Fils & Vibert.

Today, Victorian bamboo furniture enchants with its spirit of originality and daintiness, which at the time was advertised as suitable for "tasteful" English people. The ingenuity of the interwoven canework and woven grass matting, and its brightly lacquered panels, blend perfectly with most interiors to generate a quaintly exotic look.

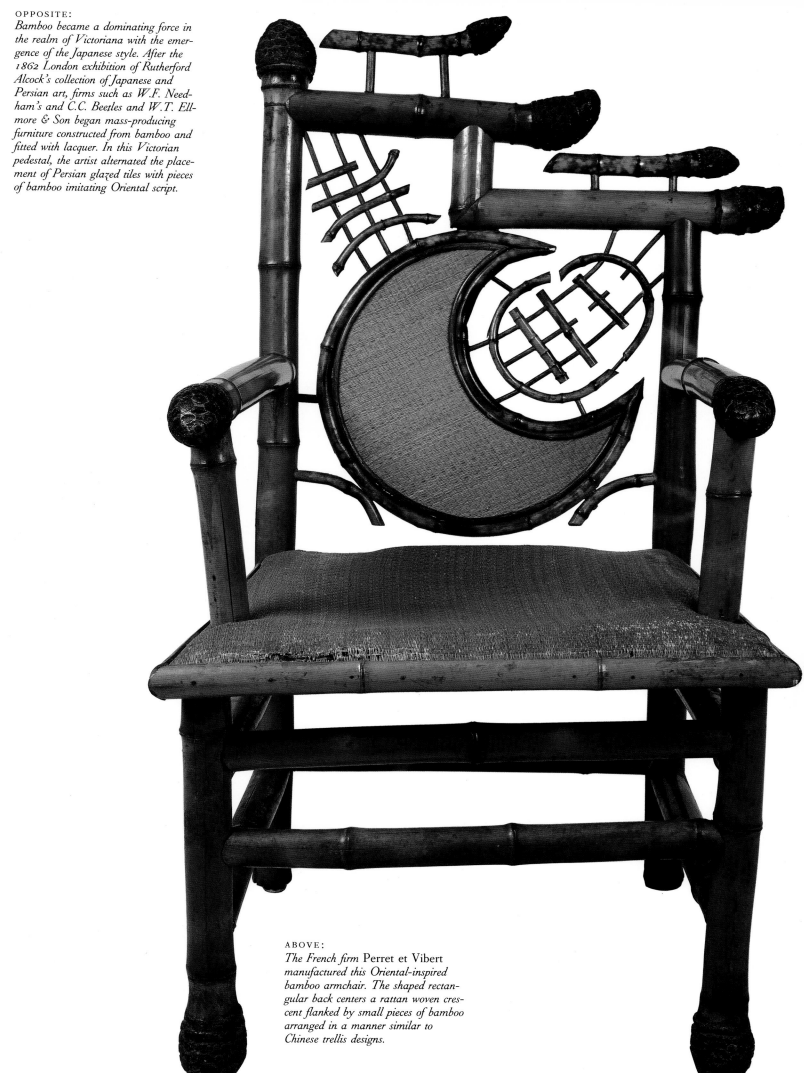

OPPOSITE:
Bamboo became a dominating force in the realm of Victoriana with the emergence of the Japanese style. After the 1862 London exhibition of Rutherford Alcock's collection of Japanese and Persian art, firms such as W.F. Needham's and C.C. Beetles and W.T. Ellmore & Son began mass-producing furniture constructed from bamboo and fitted with lacquer. In this Victorian pedestal, the artist alternated the placement of Persian glazed tiles with pieces of bamboo imitating Oriental script.

ABOVE:
The French firm Perret et Vibert manufactured this Oriental-inspired bamboo armchair. The shaped rectangular back centers a rattan woven crescent flanked by small pieces of bamboo arranged in a manner similar to Chinese trellis designs.

OPPOSITE:
Suitable for outdoor use, this late-nineteenth-/early-twentieth-century wrought-iron fernery is an example of a utilitarian item created from an industrial material. Rococo-inspired consoles and plant stands were frequently painted and decorated with foliage motifs. This example may have once been part of an ensemble of terrace furnishings.

Metal

ABOVE:
This simple wrought-iron armchair has been lavishly upholstered in multicolored crinkled fabric by the Parisian designer Yves Martahelot. The circular back and legs are wrapped with folded strips of linen and silk; the seat, similarly upholstered, sports a fabric rose.

ABOVE:
This French fire screen takes the form of a woman dressed for a ball. The shaped diadem placed around a 1920s bob hairdo attests to its production during the Art Deco period.

Preferred for centuries by architects for its qualities of durability and strength, cast iron was considered only in the late 1800s as a possible material for freestanding furniture. In their 1790s pattern book, whose title rivaled the text in length—*Ornamental Iron Work, or Designs in the Present Taste, for Fan-lights, Staircase Railing, Window-guard-irons, lamp-irons, Palisades, and Gates. With a Scheme for adjusting Designs with facility and accuracy to any shape*...—I. & J. Taylor offered suggestions for its implementation within, as well as on, the home. Acceptance was gradual, however, and J. C. Loudon's *Encyclopedia of Cottage, Farm, and Villa Architecture and Furniture,* published in 1833, included only two cast-iron chair models. At the time handwrought iron, fashioned by a blacksmith with hammer and anvil as it had been since medieval days, was considered far superior aesthetically to the cast variety, which was heavier and poorly detailed. In addition, although cast iron was unquestionably strong, it contained impurities and was brittle. It had therefore been used almost exclusively for architectural elements such as balustrades, verandas, gates, wall brackets, and fanlights, and on the hearth, for stoves and andirons.

The industrial revolution elevated cast iron's fortunes. For mass production, a poured material was preferable to one wrought individually by hand. Technological advances brought further benefits. In the 1840s access to anthracite and bituminous coal deposits revolutionized the iron industry. One improvement was that the molten liquid flowed more easily, allowing founders to achieve sharper definition in their casting.

Notwithstanding its enhanced status, cast iron drew the criticism of the foremost Victorian arbiters of taste, especially Ruskin, who, in his 1849 *Seven Lamps of Architecture,* wrote:

No ornaments . . . are so cold, clumsy, and vulgar, so essentially incapable of a fine line or shadow, as those of cast iron; and while, on the score of truth, we can hardly allege any thing against them, since they are always distinguishable, at a glance, from wrought and hammered work, and stand only for what they are, yet I feel very strongly that there is no hope of the progress of the arts of any nation which indulges in these vulgar and cheap substitutes for real decoration.

Cast iron was found guilty by association. A product of industry, mass production, and popular taste, it stood against everything Ruskin, Morris, and their disciples in the Arts and Crafts movement upheld as sacred. It did, though, achieve a fairly substantial market in garden and veranda seat furniture and fern-stands in the United Kingdom and America, for which it competed with wicker. Manufacturers such as Walter MacFarlane & Company of Glasgow, the Carron Company near Falkirk, and Hutchinson

& Wickersham in the United States offered a range of Gothic, rococo, and Renaissance revival models, in addition to some decorated with rustic and floral ornamentation. Models by the Coalbrookdale Company such as "fern" and "lily of the valley," for example, catered to the Victorian's preoccupation with nature.

Today, cast iron would appear to be an unlikely Victorian choice for outdoor furniture. Although impervious to the most unrelenting English winter, it appears awkward, cold, and uncomfortable. Even the frequent attempt to disguise its origins by the application of green paint or a bronzed patina is unconvincing.

OPPOSITE AND TOP RIGHT:
This Swedish cast-iron center table dates to the late nineteenth century and was made by the firm of J & S C.G. Bolinger of Stockholm. The reticulated circular scalloped top is cast with a profusion of scrolls on a trellis ground and set with reserves depicting the signs of the zodiac. Its designer had the sense to pierce the top, which enables rain to quickly flow through, thereby preventing the metal from rusting.

RIGHT:
Cast iron was well suited to become a popular medium for creating garden furniture in the rustic mode. One frequently cast pattern is seen in this American branch-form armchair. Possibly manufactured by the firm Hutchinson & Wickersham of New York between 1860 and 1900, this weatherbeaten chair has stretchers appropriately cast in the form of a pair of entwined garden snakes.

ABOVE:
Probably the most popular design for cast-iron garden furniture, this fern-decorated armchair evokes the feeling of walking through a dew-laden woodland forest.

Papier-Mâché

Despite its French derivation, the term *papier-mâché* describes a technique associated essentially with the English Midlands. The term is further misleading in that not all papier-mâché was comprised of mashed or pulped paper, as a direct translation implies; much of it was constructed from compressed layers of sheet paper which, from the late eighteenth century, were preferred as the manufacture of papier-mâché items expanded from a thriving Georgian enterprise into a giant Victorian industry. In 1772 Henry Clay, who had served his apprenticeship in the tinware trade in Birmingham, introduced a "new improved Paper-Ware" from sheets of paper pasted together, which could be "sawn, planed, dove-tailed, or mitred in the same manner as if made of wood." Clay used his invention to make panels for coaches, trays, and furniture. Sheet paper proved itself to be a viable substitute for both metal and wood as it was durable, malleable, inexpensive, and light.

Clay applied the same japanned decoration to his laminated papier-mâché as that used on metal by the Midlands tinware, or "Pontypool," trade, and by the late 1800s his success had secured him the patronage of Queen Charlotte, George III, and the Prince of Wales. After 1802, on the expiration of his patent and his relocation to London, Clay was succeeded in Birmingham and nearby Wolverhampton by roughly thirty-five papier-mâché japanners, including Jennens & Bettridge (1816–1864), Small & Son (1802–1816), and Woodward & Midgeley (1830–1857). Of these, Jennens & Bettridge, who purchased Clay's factory, became the most celebrated and prolific papier-mâché manufacturers in England, producing a wide range of household accessories and bric-a-brac: pole screens, inkstands, tea caddies, toiletry items, and, especially, trays.

Around 1840 Jennens & Bettridge began to experiment with furniture. Their progress was noted in the official catalogue of the 1851 Crystal Palace Exhibition: "It is not many years since the limits of the trade were circumscribed to a tea-tray, but now we find articles of furniture, not only of a slight and ornamental character, such as ladies' worktables or boxes, but of a more substantial kind, in chairs and sofas for the drawing-room, or the entire casings of pianofortes." The firm retained leading artists and designers to decorate its more ambitious pieces.

Papier-mâché was initially comprised of a mix of ingredients such as cotton and linen rags, straw, and vegetable fibers, blended with a binder of glue or gum arabic to form a pulped substance that could be fed through rollers to achieve a uniform thickness. After drying, this was molded into a predetermined form, which was then trimmed and waterproofed with a coat of linseed oil in preparation for being sent to the decorating depart-

OPPOSITE AND ABOVE:
This Victorian sewing basket, circa 1860, is one of many chinoiserie-decorated papier-mâché items made in England during the nineteenth century. Papier-mâché was an inexpensive substitute for costly Chinese-export lacquer; hence, Victorian drawing rooms were frequently filled with furnishings like this piece, attributed to the premier firm of Jennens & Bettridge.

ment. The process anticipated a host of comparable twentieth-century die-stamping processes in the fields of plastics and laminated plywoods.

The introduction of sheet paper began to phase out the pulping technique by the early 1800s. Whichever process was used, it was sometimes necessary to reinforce the finished panels with a central core of wood or iron. Chairs and tables, for example, often required additional strength in their feet or pedestal bases.

The undecorated papier-mâché blanks were now ready to be "japanned" with a high-gloss paint that imitated the expensive, onerous, and dangerous oriental technique of lacquering, from whose country of origin the technique drew its name. By 1770 japanning had become an integral part of the metal trade in Birmingham, its high-gloss ebonized finish imparting a rich sheen to the bulk of the region's metalware products. In so doing, it provided coach painters with a durable weatherproof coating. Comprised of a mix of amber, linseed oil, and asphaltum thinned with turpentine, japan varnish was produced almost universally in jet black, although burgundy, dark green, and brown were also used.

In the larger factories, papier-mâché decorators sat at long tables, applying a mix of fashionable ornamentation. Particularly popular were copies of Old Master landscapes by Landseer, Stubbs, Sanby, Morland, and Kauffmann, a mix of allegorical figures, such as the muses of poetry and music, and depictions of England's great military triumphs. Images were usually framed in neoclassical borders enhanced with dentils and Greek key motifs painted in a gold alloy that resembled lacquer. In 1842 a cheap method of transfer printing, introduced by one George Goodman of Birmingham, mechanized and vulgarized the process, as did the transfer of colored engravings in place of hand-painted decoration. These framed compositions yielded gradually to all-over floral decoration that incorporated fountains, birds of paradise, and, in an inspired version of the chinoiserie designs introduced by Jennens & Bettridge in 1821, figures, willows, and pagodas in naturalistic settings. Many of these were decorated by artists from the Wolverhampton tinware industry.

Papier-mâché decoration was greatly enhanced from around 1825 by the introduction of mother-of-pearl, which was embedded into the varnish before it fully dried. Sections of nautilus or abalone shell were pressed into the design and then covered with protective coats of translucent varnish. The shells' shimmering rainbow iridescence brought an added opulence and allure to the depiction of subjects such as historical buildings, including Windsor Castle and Westminster Abbey. Mother-of-pearl was also widely popular for a wide range of Victorian collectibles, such as buttons, buckles, and Loo, an eighteenth-century parlor game. Today, in London's East End, Pearly Kings, dressed in jackets festooned with mother-of-pearl buttons, carry on this Victorian tradition.

By 1860 papier-mâché was outmoded, although some firms, such as McCallum & Hodson (1846–1920), lingered on beyond 1900. Today it is admired, especially for its beautiful and whimsical decoration.

ABOVE:
This papier-mâché folk figure of an acrobat resembles the mechanical automatons popular in France and Switzerland from 1860 to 1900. The figure, possibly a street performer, raises himself effortlessly from a pole set in a four-legged stand. His clothing also dates to the nineteenth century.

OPPOSITE AND ABOVE LEFT:
Typically Victorian and attributed to McCallum and Hudson, this papier-mâché armchair is inset with mother-of-pearl and painted to depict a romantic landscape dotted with figures and Gothic ruins. Most papier-mâché furniture dates from the middle to the late nineteenth century and draws its inspiration from earlier rococo forms.

Bentwood

The sinuous and airy qualities of bentwood furniture stand in stark contrast to the generous scale and embellishment that characterize most nineteenth-century furniture. Its enduring popularity is due to the fact that it is functional, relatively inexpensive, and suitable for mass production—qualities that together provided the impetus for the development of the technology for this century's furniture phenomenon, tubular steel.

Credit goes almost single-handedly to Michael Thonet for the perfection of the bentwood process. Born in Boppard-am-Rhein, Prussia, in 1796, Thonet left his father's tanning business in 1819 to set up his own cabinet shop, of which he was both proprietor and sole craftsman. For more than ten years he applied himself painstakingly to the conventional production of carved and joined furniture, but around 1830 he began to experiment with thin veneers that he added to conceal the secondary woods he used in his chair production. He discovered that laminated strips of veneer, held together with glue and then placed in a warm wooden mold, could be shaped into curved back rails and headboards for chairs and beds. Refinements led, in 1836, to Thonet's first bentwood chair models, which incorporated elements of both laminated and solid wood.

Further improvements simplified and shortened Thonet's furniture production cycle as parts were integrated and new structural solutions found. An early client was Prince von Metternich, chancellor of the Austro-Hungarian empire, who encouraged Thonet to move to Vienna in 1842 with the promise of imperial patronage. In the same year Thonet was granted a patent for his bentwood process, which protected him from direct competition for the next twenty-seven years. Ten years later he applied for a further patent "for his method of giving wood various curves and forms by cutting and regluing . . . "

Assisted now by four of his five sons, Thonet turned his hand to mass production. Further invention, in the form of a steel strap which could be clamped around solid pieces of wood to bend them, expanded his output by further lowering time and costs. A factory was open in Koritschan, a small village in the heart of the Moravian forest, to help meet the increased, and now international, demand for his furniture. The firm's first catalogue, published in 1859, offered twenty-six items, many of which, with minor refinements, remained in production into the twentieth century.

Initially, Europe's bourgeoisie reacted with apprehension to bentwood's modest appearance; something more substantial—and expensive—was needed to establish one's place in society. Many of Thonet's

With the advent of the steam engine, industrialized nations began producing machine-made furniture in quantity. This Austrian bentwood settee, made by the firm of Thonet, is typical of the thousands of bentwood furnishings made in the nineteenth and early twentieth centuries. Thonet was granted a patent for his bentwood process in 1842.

early commissions came, therefore, from commercial sources, such as restaurants, cafés, and hotels. The Cafe Daum in Vienna and the Hotel zur Königin von England in Budapest helped to make bentwood furniture fashionable, as, later, did Josef Hoffmann's inclusion of bentwood chairs in the Purkersdorf sanatorium and Cabaret Fledermaus.

Michael Thonet was not the only, or first, cabinetmaker to experiment with the bentwood technique—the achievements of the Belgian Jean-Joseph Chapius and the American Samuel Gragg are always listed in studies of the industry's origins—but he was by far the most persistent and, finally, the most successful. The expiration of his bentwood patent in 1869 opened the floodgates to the host of competitors who quickly emerged. Most of these generated close, if not exact, copies of Thonet models with impunity. In some cases, even the firm's model numbers were retained. One newcomer, the Original Austrian Bentwood Furniture Company, had the effrontery in its advertisements to warn against imitations!

The firm of J. & J. Kohn evolved into Thonet's most serious challenger. Founded in 1850 by Jacob Kohn as a Moravian lumber concern, the firm had grown by 1867, when Jacob entered into a formal partnership with his son, Josef, into one with 3,000 employees. It continued to prosper, especially from the turn of the century, when a gifted young modernist, Gustav Siegel, joined the firm's design department. With Siegel's encouragement, the Secession's leading architects and designers, including Otto Wagner, Alfred Loos, Josef Hoffmann, Koloman Moser, and Marcel Kammerer, had many of their bentwood furniture designs executed by J. & J. Kohn. Also in Vienna, D. G. Fischel Sohne provided a similar range of bentwood models.

Thonet's competition was not limited to Austria. An army of bentwood manufacturers—in 1893 the number was listed at fifty-two—stretched from Russia to the Low Countries by World War I. Notable in Germany were the firms of Alsfelder Möbelfabrik in Alsfeld, Andrecht & Kruger in Kassel, and Oderfelder Fabrik in Oderfeld. In Belgium, L. & H. Cambrier *fréres,* and Herman *fréres* & Carton were similarly prominent. Today, the furniture produced by most of these enterprises appears indistinguishable—it all tends to have a distinctly "Thonet" look. In addition, most pieces are unsigned, causing difficulty in attribution.

A far different use for laminated wood was developed across the Atlantic, where a German immigrant, John Henry Belter, established his cabinetry shop in New York City around 1844. Belter applied plywood laminates so that the grain of each piece was placed at right angles to the one adjacent to it, thereby compounding the material's structural

BELOW:
This nineteenth century Thonet rocking chair is uniquely upholstered with tooled leather. The design on the back features Art Nouveau foliage and a medallion depicting a young maiden. The seat and armrests are decorated with a stylized trellis motif.

OPPOSITE:
Michael Thonet, the founder of the firm responsible for this bentwood cheval glass, is considered to be one of the most creative and successful furniture designers of all time. He pioneered the mass production of standardized furniture and by 1871 had factories throughout the world, which produced upwards of 4,000 pieces of furniture a day. This is one of his masterpieces.

strength. In 1858 he was awarded a patent for his manner of using several cauls simultaneously to bend laminated veneers. Most of his furniture was comprised of four or five layers of wood, although his most ambitious pieces included more than ten. Solid sections of wood, used mostly for chair and sofa arms and crests, were applied with a selection of the firm's deeply carved and pierced decoration. Belter's style conformed to the mid-Victorians' preoccupation with oversized and overornamented furnishings. Luxuriant floral compositions, rendered in a vigorous rococo revival style, characterized much of his bentwood production, which was often upholstered in tufted velvet.

Also in New York, the firm of John and Joseph Meeks provided brisk competition for Belter in a selection of more restrained rococo- and Renaissance-style furnishings. The wares of both firms today appear overly romantic and slightly gauche, bringing to mind the critic who described Belter's parlor suite at the 1876 Philadelphia Exhibition as "Louisiana bordello."

Despite its normal restraint, bentwood can at times be fanciful, witty, and playful. The undulating or scrolled patterns on some pieces, repeated in symmetrical bands, impart a lively look to even the most utilitarian pieces of household furniture.

ABOVE:
The scrolled supports on this bentwood plant stand identify it as one of Michael Thonet's innovative designs.

BELOW:
A late-nineteenth-century caned chaise longue, manufactured in Vienna by the Thonet firm, is but one of the many domestic products the company manufactured for middle-class consumption. In this chaise, the caned back is hinged and attached to an adjustable support structure.

Afterword

"How do you know what to collect?" the young woman, who was photographing some of our nineteenth-century majolica, asked, as she peered about in our parlor at the accretions of what can be loosely designated Victoriana.

"What kind of dumb question is that?" I almost snapped. But I did not snap. I said, "You just know. Sometimes you know right away. Sometimes it takes time. It reaches out to you. You reach out to it."

When I was a very little boy, some tattered books, in pale, buffish-colored paper, oh so old looking, reached out to me from a raggle-taggle pushcart. I got those books, Fanny Burney's *Evelina* in two Tauchnitz volumes, with a nickel scrounged from an unwilling grandfather. He had his acquisitive eye on a cut-glass bowl whose singular splendor he sensed beneath the grime encrusting it. We both loved things. This is a passion that is in our blood. And that brings me to Bruce Newman and this prodigious treasure trove of a book. Bruce and I are blood brothers. We have an identical passion in our veins: We lust for things. But Bruce has made a triumphant, lifelong career out of his lust, as his father did before him, while I have managed only a little amateur nibble here and there. *Fantasy Furniture* is a superb monument to Bruce Newman: to his highly individual taste, to his acumen, and to his love affair with craftsmanship and quality, with the eccentric, the imaginative, the improbable, and the unexpectedly humorous. Bruce is a romantic mad about the romantic. And, of course, his book is a revel for the likes of me, who could not possibly afford almost anything in it but who finds joy in having what he covets, if only between these covers.

I have tried to teach myself not to covet. I do not covet in museums—well, almost never . . . there is the Grinling Gibbons cravat and that luminescent *nef*, a ship upon whose deck Tristan and Isolde play at chess. Both cravat, miraculously carved of—is it lime wood?—and *nef* are,

LEFT:
This detail of a French asymmetrically shaped lyrical cheval glass, carved with a variety of rococo motifs, was made during the 1870s. The Rubenesque winged putto and the foliage exemplify attributes associated with romanticism.

alas, in the Victoria and Albert Museum in London. No sense in coveting cravat or *nef*. I do not covet my neighbor's ass, but I do covet his majolica, and if he has any "Black Forest" bears, I most certainly covet them as well. *Fantasy Furniture* devotes a whole section to them and their veraciously carved woodland associates. Now, we have in our house friends and relations of these Black Forest creatures: mother bear, baby bear, diminutive cousin bears, a bear who makes tinkling fairy-tale music. We even have Mr. Bear. But we do not have chairs fashioned of embracing bears, settles supported by antic bears, a settle back composed of a consort of bears industriously playing musical instruments, nor any of the other ursine charmers in this book. And do we covet! I could go on and on: the delicately towering art nouveau clock in the "Belle Epoque" chapter; the Belle Epoque chair intricately composed of two realistically colored giant sunflowers (not as costly as a Van Gogh, but definitely beyond our range, even paid out over the next decade). Indeed, this book teems with desirable winged or demonic creatures supporting, enhancing, lighting upon, and even *being* fabulous household furniture: dragons and devils of extraordinary charm or malignancy, double-headed phoenixes, sphinxes, satyrs, lions rampant, griffins, swans with necks of infinite sinuosity, peacocks galore, monkeys tricking and treating—one is actually seated, playing a flute! So, indeed, I do covet. But that is, as I have said, the joy of owning this book: I can have it all exuberantly between covers. And how wonderful to share a deeply personal conviction, confirmed by *Fantasy Furniture*: "maximal" is as satisfying as minimal. Too much is not enough—for, obviously, the Victorians, Bruce Newman, or, for that matter, me.

LEO LERMAN

Bibliography

FATHERS OF FANTASY

Arthaud, Claude. *Dream Palaces—Fantastic Houses and their Treasures*, London: Thames & Hudson, 1973.

Bertram, Werner. *A Royal Recluse, Memories of Ludwig II of Bavaria*, Munich: Martin Herpich & Son, Engravers & Publishers.

Blunt, Wilfrid. *The Dream King*, London: Hamish Hamilton Ltd., 1970.

Conrads, Ulrich, and Sperlich, Hans G. *The Architecture of Fantasy*, New York: Frederick A. Praeger Publishers.

Designs for the Dream King: The Castles and Palaces of Ludwig II of Bavaria, Exhibition catalogue, Victoria and Albert Museum, London: Debrett's Peerage Ltd., 1979.

Dinkel, John. *The Royal Pavilion Brighton*, London: Scala Publications, Ltd., 1983.

Manguel, Alberto, and Guadalupi, Gianni. *The Dictionary of Imaginary Places*, San Diego: Harcourt Brace Jovanovich, Publishers, 1987.

Musgrave, Clifford. *Brighton Past and Present*, London: The Stockport Express Ltd.

Roberts, Henry D. *The Royal Pavilion Brighton*, London: The Royal Pavilion Estate, Public Libraries Art Gallery, 1939.

Porphyria—A Royal Malady, London: British Medical Association, 1968.

Regency Exhibition 1956—The Royal Pavilion Brighton, London: The Dolphin Press, Ltd., 1956.

The Royal Pavilion Brighton Catalogue Centenary Festival 1850–1950, Brighton: County Borough of Brighton, 1950.

The Royal Pavilion at Brighton, London: Greenaway-Harrison Limited, 1986.

Sprange, Joseph Herbert. *The Royal Bavarian Castles in Word and Picture*, Munich: Josef Ludwig Craemer, 1904.

GROTESQUE & MYTHOLOGICAL

Aslin, Elizabeth. *19th Century English Furniture*, London: Faber Publishers, 1962.

Boe, Alf. *From Gothic Revival to Functional Form*, Oslo: University Press, 1957.

Boger, Louise Ade. *The Complete Guide to Furniture Styles*, New York: Charles Scribner's Sons, 1969.

Foley, Edwin. *The Book of Decorative Furniture, its form, color and history*, London, 1910–11.

Gloag, John. *Georgian Grace: A Social History of Design from 1660–1830*, London: A. & C. Black, 1956.

Gloag, John. *The Englishman's Chair: Origins, design and social history of seat furniture in England*, London: Allen & Unwin Publishers, 1964.

Hayward, Helena (ed.). *World Furniture*, London: Hamlyn Publishing Group Ltd., 1965.

Lighten, Frances. *Decorative Arts of Victoria's Era*, New York: Charles Scribner, 1950.

Lucas, A. *Ancient Egyptian Materials and Industries*, 4th edition, London: J.K. Harris Publishers, 1962.

Madigan, Mary Jean. *Nineteenth Century Furniture: Innovation, Revival and Reform*, New York: Art & Antiques, 1982.

Payne, Christopher. *The Price Guide to 19th Century European Furniture*, London: Antique Collector's Club, 1981.

Symonds, R.W., and Whineray, B.B. *Victorian Furniture*, London: Country Life, 1962.

BLACK FOREST

Holzschnitzerei F. Peter Trauffer Luzern Wood Carving, Buchdruckerei C.J. Bucher A.G., Luzern, n.d.

Kantonale Schnitzlerschule Brienz 1884–1984, Brienz: Peter Fluck, 1984.

Muller, Dr. B. *Der Holzbildhauer Chronologie eines Kinsthandwerks—Schnitzlerschule von 1884–1984*, Austellung im Kornhaus Bern, 1984.

HORN & ANTLER

Heckscher, Morrison. "Eighteenth-Century Rustic Furniture Designs," *Furniture History*, 1975, pp. 59–65.

Jervis, Simon. "Furniture in Horn and Antler", *Connoisseur*, London, November, 1977, pp. 190–199.

Jervis, Simon. "Antler and Horn Furniture", *Victoria & Albert Museum Yearbook*, London, #3, 1972, pp. 87–99.

St. John, Richard. *Longhorn Artist Wenzel Friedrich*, Wichita: Wichita State University, Kansas, 1982.

"The Spread of the Country Life Idea," *Country Life in America*, August 22, 1908, p. 12.

MATERIALS

Corbin, Patricia. *All About Wicker*, New York: E.P. Dutton, 1979.

"Furniture and Rural Structures of Iron," *Illustrated Annual Register of Rural Affairs*, 1858–60, pp. 153–59.

Gilborn, Craig. *Adirondack Furniture and the Rustic Tradition*, New York: Harry N. Abrams, 1987.

Harris, William Laurel. "Rustic Life and the Furniture It Demands," *Good Furniture*, October, 1915, pp. 228–32.

Hibberd, Shirley. *Rustic Adornments for Homes and Taste*, London: Groombridge & Sons, 1856.

Hibberd, Shirley. *Rustic Adornments for Houses of Taste*, 3rd edition, London: Groombridge & Sons, 1870.

Ideas for Rustic Furniture proper for Garden Seats, Summer Houses, Hermitages, Cottages, Printed for I. & J. Taylor, Architectural Library, Holborn, England, 1785–90.

Malcles, Laurent. "Meubles Noirs en Carton Deguise," *Art et Decoration*, January, 1939, pp. 191–198.

Manwarring, Robert. *Cabinet and Chair-Maker's Real Friend and Companion*, London: Pranker, 1765; London: John Tiranti, 1937 (reprint).

Maskell, Alfred, F.S.A. *Ivories*, New York: G.P. Putnam's Sons, 1905.

Mipaas, Esther. "Cast Iron Furnishings," *American Art & Antiques*, May-June, 1979, pp. 34–41.

"On Rustic-work as Garden Ornaments," *The Gardener's Magazine*, 1834, pp. 485–89.

Ostergard, Derek E. (ed.). *Bent Wood and Metal Furniture: 1850–1946*, Seattle: The University of Washington Press, 1987.

"Rustic Adornments," *The Gardener's Monthly*, November, 1860, pp. 320, 338–39.

Saunders, Richard. *Collecting & Restoring Wicker Furniture*, New York: Crown Publishers, Inc., 1976.

Saunders, Richard. *Heywood Brothers & Wakefield Company Classic Wicker Furniture: The Complete 1898–1899 Illustrated Catalog*, New York: Dover Publications, 1982.

Scott, W. B. *Ornamental Designs for Furniture and House Decoration*, Edinburgh: A. Fullanton & Co.

Snyder, Ellen Maire. "Victory over Nature: Victorian Cast-Iron Seating Furniture," *Winterthur Portfolio*, no. 4, 1985.

Stephenson, Sue Honaker. *Rustic Furniture*, New York: Van Nostrand Reinhold, 1979.

Toller, Jane. "Colorful Variety in Papier-Mache Furniture," *The Antique Dealer and Collectors Guide*, November, 1970, pp. 72–75.

Von Erdberg, Eleanor. *Chinese Influences on European Garden Structures*, Cambridge, Massachusetts: Harvard University Press, 1936.

Walking, Gillian. *Antique Bamboo Furniture*, London: Bell & Hyman Ltd., 1979.

Walking, Gillian. "Papier Mache," *The Connoisseur*, July 1980, Vol. 204, pp. 222–227.

Ward-Jackson, P. *English Furniture Designs of the Eighteenth Century*, London, 1958.

GROTTO

Echenique, Amalio Huarte Y. *Guia de Salamanca*, Salamanca: Libreria De Antonio Garcia, 1920.

Himmelheber, Georg. "Die Sonderbaren Grottenmobel," *Weltkunst*, No. 53, 1983, pp. 202–209.

Himmelheber, Georg. "Die Geliebten Grottenmobel," *Weltkunst*, 1 Dezember, 1983, pp. 3433–3436.

Konkylien og Mennesket, Udstilling i Kunstindustrimuseet, Kobenhavn, 25 November 1983–15 January 1984, Germany, 1984.

Miller, Naomi. *Heavenly Caves Reflections on the Garden Grotto*, New York: George Braziller, 1982.

Seulliet, Philippe, "Le Chateau du Sorcier," *Decoration Internationale*, no. 57, Decembre, 1982, pp. 101–110.

Stix, Hugh and Marguerite, and Abbot, R. Tucker. *The Shell: Five Hundred Million Years of Inspired Design*, New York: Harry N. Abrams, 1968.

BELLE EPOQUE

Amayo, Mario. *Art Nouveau*, London: Studio Vista, 1966.

Art Nouveau: Art and Design at the Turn of the Century, exhibition catalogue, The Museum of Modern Art, New York, 1959.

Duncan, Alastair. *Art Nouveau Furniture*, London: Thames & Hudson, Ltd., 1982.

Galle, exhibition catalogue, Musee du Luxembourg, Paris, 29 novembre 1985–2 fevrier 1986, Editions de la Reunion des Musees Nationaux, Paris, 1985.

Graham, F. Lanier. *Hector Guimard*, Exhibition catalogue, The Museum of Modern Art, New York, 1970.

Julian, Philippe. *The Triumph of Art Nouveau Paris Exhibition 1900*, London: Phaidon Press Ltd., 1974.

L'Oeuvre de Rupert Carabin, 1862–1932, Exhibition catalogue, Galerie de Luxembourg, Paris, 1974.

Madsen, Stephen Tschudi. *Sources of Art Nouveau*, New York: G. Wittenborn, 1916.

Credits

The objects presented in this book are the property of Newel Art Galleries, Inc., New York, and have been photographed by Dan Rubin and Stuart Friedman, with the exception of the following objects and photographs from other sources listed here according to the pages on which they appear in this book:

pp. 8–9: Photograph Courtesy of Carlton Hobbs.

p. 10: Photograph courtesy of the Art Gallery and Museums and The Royal Pavilion, Brighton.

pp. 12–13: Photograph courtesy of Martin Herpich & Son Engravers & Printers, Munich.

pp. 14–15 (top left and bottom right): Photographs courtesy of Scala Publications Ltd. First published in *The Royal Pavilion* by J.M.A. Dinkel.

p. 14–15 (center): Photograph courtesy of the Art Gallery and Museums and The Royal Pavilion, Brighton.

pp. 17–19: Photographs courtesy of the Art Gallery and Museums and The Royal Pavilion, Brighton.

p. 20: Photographs courtesy of the Museumverwaltung, Schloss Nymphenburg, Munich.

p. 21: Photograph courtesy of Martin Herpich & Son Engravers & Publishers, Munich.

pp. 22–23: Photographs courtesy of the Museumverwaltung, Schloss Nymphemburg, Munich.

p. 34 (Bottom): Collection of Mr. and Mrs. Bruce M. Newman.

p. 39: Collection of Barbara and Maurizio Berger.

p. 40 (top left): Photograph courtesy of G.T. Ratcliff Ltd.

p. 47: Collection of Mr. and Mrs. Bruce M. Newman.

pp. 66–67: Photograph by François Halard.

pp. 68–69: Collection of Barbara and Maurizio Berger.

p. 75: Collection of Marianna Vardinayannis.

p. 88 (top): Collection of Thorunn Wathne.

pp. 92–93: Photograph by François Halard.

pp. 106, 108: Collections of C. Douglas Dillon and Mr. and Mrs. Gordon Gray.

p. 131: Collection of Barbara and Maurizio Berger.

pp. 132–133: Collection of Dr. and Mrs. Michael Greenwald.

p. 134: Photographs courtesy of Mallett at Bourdon House Ltd.

p. 135: Photograph courtesy of *Vogue Decoration*, Paris. Collection of Mony Linz Einstein.

pp. 136–137: Photograph courtesy of the Musee de l'Ecole de Nancy.

p. 141 (bottom right): Collection of Warner LeRoy.

p. 144 (top left): Collection of Mr. and Mrs. Bruce M. Newman.

p. 145: Photograph courtesy of the Maison Soubrier.

p. 147 (right): Collection of Mr. and Mrs. G.G. Beckwith Gilbert.

pp. 148–149: Photograph courtesy of *Vogue Decoration*, Paris.

p. 154: Photograph courtesy of the Musee des Beaux-Arts, Strasbourg.

p. 155: Private Collection.

p. 156: Photograph courtesy of the Reunion des Musee Nationaux, Paris.

p. 157: Photograph courtesy of the Musee D'Orsay, Paris.

p. 160 (top right): Photograph courtesy of Jean-Loup Charmet.

p. 161 (bottom right): Collection of Donna and Dick Soloway.

pp. 162–163: Collection of Mr. and Mrs. Tom Watson.

p. 166 (left): Collection of Michel Ottin.

pp. 166–167 (center): Collection of Roberto Polo.

p. 193: Collection of Brooke and Peter Duchin.

Acknowledgments

Gratitude is extended to the following in the compilation of this book:

MaryBeth McCaffrey for her research; Ray Perman of the Grosvenor Gallery; Simon Jervis of the Victoria and Albert Museum; Craig Gilborn of the Adirondack Museum; Ursula Trauffer; and Andrea Fiuczynski.

For their assistance in providing photographs: Jessica Rutherford and Cynthia Campbell at The Royal Pavilion at Brighton; Jean-Loup Charmet; Suzanne Dalton and François Hallard, Paris; John Steel at the Antique Collectors' Club Ltd., London; Dr. Schloss of the Museumsverwaltung, Schloss Nymphenburg, Munich; John York of Mallett at Bourdon House Ltd.; Wendy Ratcliff; Carlton and John Hobbs; Michel Ottin; the Soubrier family; *Vogue Decoration*, Paris; Christie's, London; and Sotheby's, London.

For their outstanding photography: Dan Rubin and Stuart Friedman.

For their time and enthusiasm: Lewis Baer, who gave me particular motivation; Mildred Males; George Richard Szepinski; Doreen Decaminada; Ruben DeSaavedra; and Larry Sirolli.

And to the following people who, without hesitancy, gave of their talents: Tom Hoving, John L. Marion, John Loring, Marvin D. Schwartz, Stanley Marcus; Leo Lerman, Sister Parish, and Erté.

Finally, very special thanks go to Alastair Duncan, for his advice on embarking on this project; to Charles Davey for his creative design concept; and to Robert Janjigian, my editor, whose professionalism surfaced during every meeting.